Morgan

After a long and satisfying process here is the finished product.

Thank you for your help & support!

Your friend

John

ADVANCE PRAISE

"As I read *The Entrepreneurial Journey*, so many of the stories and lessons resonated with my own experiences building DICK'S Sporting Goods. This incredible resource unwinds the complexities of raising capital and building and managing a team like no other book I've read. I wish I had read this earlier!"

—**Ed Stack**, Chairman and CEO of DICK'S Sporting Goods

"As an entrepreneur, I appreciate business owners who harness their own ideas and turn them into successful companies. *The Entrepreneurial Journey* is a must-read for anyone who is thinking of starting a business! It is one of the best books out there and will provide tangible advice like no other."

—**Robert A. Crown**, Founder, Chairman, President, and CEO, Crown Communications, Inc.; Founder, Crown Castle International; Chairman, President, and CEO, Crown Castle USA

"For those just starting out to those preparing to sell, the insights John pulls from his experience and from those of his clients are priceless."

—**Morgan O'Brien,** President and CEO of Peoples Natural Gas

"*The Entrepreneurial Journey* takes a deep dive into the personal issues entrepreneurs will have to manage when they make their own leap of faith to try and build their businesses. This book focuses precisely on those critically important emotions that can make or break your business."

—**Dave Stern**, President and CEO of Paris Companies

"As an entrepreneur and professor at Babson College, I was always searching for books to help my students, colleagues, and friends pursue their own entrepreneurial journeys. John Waldron's book is just such a resource. Read it, and then create your own opportunity!"

—**Dr. John W. Altman**, Professor and Trustee Emeritus, Miami University of Ohio; Chairman, John W. Altman Charitable Foundation

"Most business owners maintain a team of professionals to address the financial, tax, and legal issues they will invariably encounter, but a business psychologist is not usually on that team. *The Entrepreneurial Journey* does a wonderful job of identifying and diagnosing the emotional challenges one is likely to face—from launch to maturation and growth, and ultimately, to sale."

—**Dick Wiley**, Cofounder, Wiley Rein, LLP; former Chairman, Federal Communications Commission

"John takes us on a insightful journey into how to be successful, not only as a entrepreneur, but as a business leader and a person. His linkage of Emotional Intelligence to creating sustainable value for customers, stakeholders, and oneself is foundational to success in any business and in life. *The Entrepreneurial Journey* is a must-read."

—**Richard J. Harshman**, Retired Chairman, President and CEO, Allegheny Technologies Incorporated

The Entrepreneurial
JOURNEY

The Entrepreneurial
JOURNEY

Navigating a Successful Path
for Your Business, Family, and Future

JOHN J. WALDRON

RIVER GROVE
BOOKS

Published by River Grove Books
Austin, TX
www.rivergrovebooks.com

Distributed by River Grove Books

Design and composition by Greenleaf Book Group and Kim Lance
Cover design by Greenleaf Book Group and Kim Lance
Cover images used under license from ©iStockphoto.com/alzav

Publisher's Cataloging-in-Publication data is available.

Paperback ISBN: 978-1-63299-250-5

Hardcover ISBN: 978-1-63299-249-9

eBook ISBN: 978-1-63299-251-2

Printed in the United States of America on acid-free paper

19 20 21 22 23 24   10 9 8 7 6 5 4 3 2 1

First Edition

To my wife, Maureen; my children, Shea, Bryan, and Michael;
my clients; and my second family,
my team members at Waldron Private Wealth

And to all of those future entrepreneurs who
choose to believe in themselves and go all in on their dreams

NEVER HAS THE FOLLOWING STATEMENT BEEN MORE TRUE

THAN IN THE ENTREPRENEURIAL JOURNEY:

"IF IT WERE EASY, EVERYONE WOULD DO IT."

Contents

Preface

ENTREPRENEURS GET TO ENJOY one of the most exciting and challenging journeys this country has to offer. And while the rewards are high, the probability of success is quite low. This is why scholars, universities, and even entire schools dedicate significant resources to examining the processes, people, skills, and trends that can contribute to an equation for entrepreneurial success. Everyone's looking for that magic formula so they may succeed where others fail. What qualities propel some entrepreneurs to success, or at least increase the probability of their success? And why is the failure rate so high?

Unlike those scholars and universities who approach this elusive formula from an academic and historical perspective, I have had the privilege of working with hundreds of entrepreneurs in the trenches, in real time, as they make decisions and take actions that determine the ultimate outcome of their venture. What I have found is this: Academic and historical perspectives gloss over the crucial and ever-present intangibles, such as passion, inner drive, leadership, self-awareness, and self-control, that exist in successful entrepreneurs. This is where most theories fall short, because it is those intangibles that great entrepreneurs lean on during the most pivotal moments of decisive action.

As this book will show, the intangibles have every bit as much (and perhaps more) influence on the outcome as the tangibles. Further, no matter what phase of the business lifecycle you find yourself in, this book will provide you with invaluable insights gathered from my decades of experience working with successful *and* unsuccessful entrepreneurs. If we imagine that running a business is like navigating a ship across the ocean, then this book will help you weather the many storms and identify those hidden icebergs that threaten to sink your venture.

As you travel on your own entrepreneurial journey, this book will help you manage the intertwining issues you will face, including the increasing value of your enterprise; the demands and expectations from the multitude of stakeholders you will collect along the way; the increasing complexity of personal wealth management that becomes inevitable as a result of your success; the interrelated and often complicated family and wealth dynamics; succession planning; and, most importantly, how to manage your own emotions (and keep your sanity) through all the phases of a successful entrepreneurial journey.

The formula for success is one that properly balances the tangible issues—like creating and producing a unique product or service, financing the business, structuring solid tax and legal entities, formulating an effective sales strategy, and so on—with the intangible qualities that lead to entrepreneurial success. With that balance, we can better identify what drives the entrepreneur to pursue his or her passion so relentlessly without being deterred by negative external influences or by the haunting emotions of doubt, fear, anxiety, and insecurity. You will find no shortage of resources that outline the tangible influences on entrepreneurial success, but we will examine the many ways that managing those invisible, intangible elements can make all the difference.

Emotional Intelligence Is Key

Traditional thinking suggests that the path is supposed to look like this: You're born with a certain IQ, you go to college and study hard, and then you use that IQ and enhanced knowledge to achieve your dreams. So why

is it that many entrepreneurs achieve great success despite being scholastically average? There's a tendency to describe this phenomenon with
terms like "street smarts" or "charisma." But now, thanks to technological
advancement and years of research by professional psychologists, we have
arrived at a more scientific term: Emotional Intelligence (EI).

With his best-selling book *Emotional Intelligence: Why It Can Matter
More Than IQ*, Dr. Daniel Goleman explains that recent improvements
in brain imaging technology allow us to collect mountains of neurologi-
cal data on emotional extremes, pivot triggers, and how the brain center
moves us from emotion to emotion.[1] This breakthrough led to a pre-
ponderance of studies about how EI influences the human condition.
Today you can find a book that applies the science to just about every
aspect of life, from personal relationships to professional leadership to
sales techniques to happiness and well-being.

While this book is not specifically about Emotional Intelligence,
its principles are certainly rooted in the science. As the founder and
CEO of a business that counsels hundreds of successful entrepreneurs,
I've often pondered the central question posed by Dr. Goleman's book:
Why do business leaders with high IQs sometimes falter or stagnate
while those with average IQs sometimes achieve great accomplishments? Then there's the follow-up question: When our feelings so often
trump reality—when we have emotional habits and impulses that are
sometimes difficult to control—how do we achieve the perfect balance
between IQ and EI? Finally, we arrive at the ultimate question: What is
the equation for entrepreneurial success?

This book answers those questions. However, it is *not* a book that
will tell you how to become the next Steve Jobs, Jeff Bezos, or Bill Gates.
If I could do that, then my name would be listed alongside theirs. What
I will do is seek to provide the answers for how to be a more emotionally

---

1   Daniel Goleman, *Emotional Intelligence: Why It Can Matter More Than IQ* (New York: Bantam, 1995).

intelligent entrepreneur, business leader, and business grower through-out the typical lifecycle of a successful business. By leaning on the personal experience and real-world evidence provided by the many entrepreneurs our company has worked with over the years, we arrive at a deeper understanding of how even scholastically average people can overcome substantial obstacles while balancing a growing collection of stakeholders and *leading* hundreds and sometimes even thousands of employees on a journey to build amazing businesses.

These stories will illustrate the critical role managing your emotions plays in the secret formula of entrepreneurial success. Unfortunately, as both science and experience show us, emotions have extremes. Here are a few of those extremes that you will experience *often* on your entrepreneurial journey:

- Security and fear
- Contentment and anxiousness
- Love and hate
- Admiration and jealousy
- Confidence and insecurity
- Trust and distrust
- Pity and indignation
- Joy and anger
- Generosity and greed

Why do these extremes exist? And why are they so tightly linked? Part of the answer is this: As we evolved into *Homo sapiens*, our emotions developed first, and our intellect and ability to reason didn't develop until later.[2] This is why, in extreme situations, logic flies out the window and we snap back to our instinctive emotional reactions.

---

2   Nigel Nicholson, "How Hardwired Is Human Behavior?" *Harvard Business Review*, July–August 1998, https://hbr.org/1998/07/how-hardwired-is-human-behavior.

For the entrepreneur, the problem with having this tendency baked into our DNA is that the creation of wealth and the presence of money are lightning rods for those extremes. As you're trying to manage your own anxiety and excitement, competitive edge can turn to greed, trust can turn to distrust, and joy to anger. Every good emotion has an evil twin—its precise opposite.

The first step to mitigating the damage that these extremes can cause is to understand what is happening when these emotions take hold of you. The next step is harnessing your self-control. How you manage the emotional triggers that happen along your entrepreneurial journey is a huge part of what will make or break your leadership and your business. If you can get those emotions in check, then you will be able to make better decisions that will allow your business to keep growing and improving.

As the science of EI suggests, getting your emotions in check requires empathy, self-awareness, self-control, a positive relationship with your inner voice, listening and conflict resolution, cooperation, and collaboration (which is an absolute necessity for a growing business).

With my more than twenty-five years of experience as a business owner, I have become well versed in the presence and importance of the concepts I explore in the following chapters. I have made a lot of mistakes that I have had to learn from, and I want to share that knowledge with you. And that knowledge is supplemented by the expertise of many of the business owners that our company, Waldron Private Wealth,[3] has counseled over the years. Through our combined insight and practical experience, we can provide everything you need to diagnose your business's needs, identify which emotions you are likely to be dealing with and when, learn how to get those emotions under control, and finally, understand which technical strategies will best help you overcome your challenges and grow a successful business.

---

3   Waldron Private Wealth, accessed June 21, 2019, https://www.waldronprivatewealth.com.

The Wind and the Current

IT IS NOT DIFFICULT to find a book about the technical aspects of starting, growing, and selling a business. Unfortunately, too few of them address the equally important *emotional* side. This is a problem because money and emotion share an inextricable connection.

Many of the best entrepreneurs know that they can rely on their trusted professional team to help them survive volatile financial markets, shifting economics, regulations, tax law, geopolitical disruptions, the complexities of trust law, charitable giving, philanthropy, and the changes in family relationships that come from birth, death, marriage, and in some cases, divorce. The technical advice for navigating these matters is vitally important, but it only addresses the mathematical, dollars-and-cents portion of the picture.

To see the full picture and achieve the greatest level of success, you have to balance that technical advice with something that most professional services teams *don't* bring to the table: a deeper understanding of how the advice integrates with your unique emotional composition and that of your family, partners, clients, key employees, and other stakeholders.

Balance and Precision

At its core, money is a resource, a tool for humans to provide for our most basic needs. Once we have satisfied our needs for food, water, safety, and shelter, we use our excess money and resources to satisfy our *emotional needs*. First we seek survival, and then we seek contentment. Every person's recipe for contentment is unique, even if some of the ingredients are similar. As our wealth increases, that recipe changes, and we find ourselves adding more emotional ingredients, like purpose, self-esteem, philanthropy, and legacy.

Wealth is like many other things in life: If you control it, then it can enhance your experience and bring you joy, but if you allow it to control you, it can be dangerous. Money is volatile, and it has to be handled carefully or it can set off a violent reaction in the form of the extreme emotions hardwired into our DNA. As we seek security, we must deal with fear. The path to contentment is lined with anxiety, greed, and love's evil twin, hate. For every measure of trust, there is also the potential for distrust. Joy can become anger in a heartbeat. The effort to construct a strong self-esteem comes with the risk of an inflated ego and narcissism. It's like that old board game Operation. If you don't proceed with precision, you'll set off the buzzer and lose the game.

The Evolving Complexities of Wealth

The goal, of course, is to bring our emotions into balance as we accumulate enough wealth to meet our needs. The problem is that those needs tend to evolve and become more complex over time. Often, the older we get, the more successful we become, and more people need to be added to the emotional balancing act. Spouses, ex-spouses, children, extended family members, key players in the growth of the business— they all become stakeholders whose needs and contentment we have to consider along with our own. As wealth increases, the stresses (and therefore the emotions) change and multiply, the stakes get higher, the stakeholders become more numerous, and the emotional and technical decision-making matrix grows ever more complicated.

On top of this, even if you manage to achieve balance between your emotional and technical needs, and even if you balance it precisely with the emotional and technical needs of all your stakeholders, there is still always the chance that an unexpected life event will occur and change everything. The moment you think you have your resources aligned to take care of everyone, there's a birth, or one of your children gets married. A key person you count on decides to leave or retire. A death you haven't planned for changes everyone's perspective. Or maybe it's starting to look like it's time to sell your business. Just when you think you have every-thing figured out, all the rules change, and some of the old emotions that have been on the sidelines for a while wind up getting back in the game.

There are plenty of technical strategies for navigating these life events. Unfortunately, none of them appropriately considers the way these events can trigger positive emotions like excitement, love, security, and trust, or negative emotions like fear, greed, resentment, and dis-trust. Every major change can disrupt your progression along the con-tinuum of wealth and send you reeling, with significant discomfort and unrest. If you follow the technical advice, you might fix the disruption on the financial side; but if this doesn't achieve harmony and happiness for you and all your stakeholders, then the only thing you've done is preserve some money. You haven't solved the problem.

UNTIL THIS POINT, I'VE referred to your business's leadership in the singular. I do this only to simplify the language. Not all businesses start with a single person at the helm. Some are led by partners, others by groups. Some journeys begin with the

continued

business owner(s) own money and assets on the line. Others secure bank loans, seek venture capital, or gain support from angel investors. Depending on who runs your business and where your capital comes from, the technical strategies might be different. Rest assured, I'll cover the differences in the pages to come. But no matter who runs your business and where your capital comes from, the emotional side of the picture is the same. For this reason, I will refer to you as the singular leader of your business, even if you may have partners and investors.

Depending on your situation, the business and financial planning issues that you will face might be different, but the human emotions attached to the money are all the same. In other words, if you have $1 million or $100 million, the complexity of wealth and the risks are relative, but the emotions are extremely similar. This is exactly why so many financial and business strategies don't work for *everyone*. There is no one-size-fits-all approach to starting a business and growing it to the point of sale or succession. Sure, it's easy enough to provide the technical steps to follow, but often, what is technically correct is not necessarily emotionally acceptable. The key is finding the technical path that fits within your emotional makeup.

Without a deep understanding of the connection between money and emotion, the technical advice becomes meaningless. This concept is so important to me that I chose to build my life and business around it. I believe in it so deeply that our company, Waldron Private Wealth,[4] makes a point to limit the number of clients we work with—because we recognize the importance of intimately understanding each client's unique emotional relationship with money, along with the emotional components related to their family, partners, and other stakeholders. As

4   Waldron Private Wealth, accessed June 21, 2019, https://www.waldronprivatewealth.com.

we have learned from working with many successful entrepreneurs over the years, technical advice can help stakeholders address the financial issues associated with building a business, but without the emotional consideration, there's a huge gap in awareness that can wreak havoc for any entrepreneur and any business, no matter how successful.

Genuine Experience, Practical Advice

I have been extremely fortunate in my entrepreneurial journey to work with so many brilliant clients. I have witnessed their many successes (and some failures). I even simultaneously endured the same phase of what I call the Entrepreneurial Lifecycle with some of them. With these clients, I could empathize and share my personal advice. For those clients who were ahead of me in the Lifecycle, I could share insights from the vast knowledge base our company has gathered over the years. This also gave me a vision into what lay ahead for my own personal business venture. I'm not simply theorizing on these emotional lessons and technical strategies (and their often conflicting positions); I've *lived* them (both good and otherwise).

By referencing the good decisions and many mistakes that these successful entrepreneurs made, we have been able to help hundreds of entrepreneurs diagnose the phase of the Lifecycle they're currently occupying, identify and integrate the technical solutions, and then bring to light the emotions in play at the moment. All of this works in concert to develop appropriate solutions to any problems that arise that are *technically correct* and *emotionally acceptable.* I have seen so many key decisions delayed or never made because the correct strategy just "doesn't feel right." What this means is that the strategy wasn't emotionally acceptable to the individual. Until you acknowledge this reality, finding the right solution is impossible. And there is no time to waste. Delaying in these moments can be damaging or fatal to your business.

We have invested a great deal of time, money, training, and education in understanding how the technical knowledge of wealth management intersects with the human, emotional side of the individual and their family. Without the understanding and experience of the emotional composition of the individual and family, one simply *can't* provide the optimal technical financial strategies and advice.

TWO CAVEATS HERE . . .

FIRST, JUST LIKE EVERY business is unique, so is every person. Each individual's thumbprint of happiness is completely their own. The key is to identify that special blended recipe of the emotions in play and then use that recipe to find the most happiness. At the end of the day, for the advice we all seek—whether financial, health, spiritual, or marital—the goal is to bring happiness and joy to the life of the recipients of that advice. So if we can identify that unique emotional recipe of happiness, we can then develop the optimal financial and technical strategies for your business.

Second, let's recall the points I raised in the introduction to this book: Our emotions are something we have from birth. Yes, the blend of them is unique to the individual, but we all share similar emotions. I have worked with business owners (and just as importantly, their families) across multiple industries, generations, and locations, and what I have found is that the emotions typically at play are agnostic to industry, size, geography, product, or service. Through these experiences, I have seen how combining the technical and emotional side of business and wealth can help a leader more effectively navigate the Entrepreneurial Lifecycle, no matter who that leader may be, what kind of business he or she leads, or who his or her stakeholders happen to be.

The Four Phases of the Entrepreneurial Lifecycle

You may be wondering what exactly *is* the Entrepreneurial Lifecycle I'm referring to here? The best and brightest entrepreneurs I have worked with have helped me identify the four key phases of any business:

1. Survival
2. Maturation
3. Transition
4. The Day After

SURVIVAL

In the first phase, Survival, you're usually creating or purchasing a business. These are the days, weeks, months, or years you spend figuring out how to run this business effectively. You discover what traits of yours work best as a leader, what products or services will lead to the most growth, and which people are best equipped to help you on your journey. If you approach this phase correctly, you also discover the emotions at play—all those feelings and symptoms that can either help or harm you in your effort to reach the next phase of the Lifecycle. This is where the "Survival" comes into play. You're fighting for your life. Or at least you're fighting for the life of your business, clawing and scratching simply to get from one day to the next.

MATURATION

Maturation refers to that point when your business begins to get traction and enters a steady arc of growth. There are three stages to this phase—called Early-Stage Growth, Mid-Stage Growth, and Late-Stage Growth—and with each stage comes a new layer of technical and emotional complexity. As your business grows, the more people you reach, the more stakeholders depend on you, and the more complicated it becomes to balance your business needs with your personal needs. The ideal strategy balances the technical components of carefully growing a business with the emotional side of managing a growing list of stakeholders and preparing them for the day when you finally step down as the leader.

TRANSITION

Next comes the Transition Phase, which refers to the period when you prepare to either sell your business or execute a succession plan. The strategies vary from business to business and leader to leader, but hope, anxiety, relief, and doubt are emotions that are practically universal here. For some, the Transition leads to a sense of freedom (either to pursue other business or professional opportunities or to spend more time with family or to seek out personal interests). For others, it leads only to confusion about what comes next. Self-awareness and a good strategy can help you avoid the latter.

THE DAY AFTER

The Day-After Phase is exactly what it sounds like. You've spent however many years leading your business as an entrepreneur. Your finances, your social circle, your day-to-day existence, and many other aspects of your personal and professional life (both seen and unseen) tend to get tangled up with the business itself. Now that the business isn't part of your life anymore, what in the world are you supposed to do? Where is the money going to come from? How will you entertain yourself, keep yourself engaged, and maintain the same level of joy you achieved while running your business? How will you occupy enough of your time so that your spouse—who suddenly has to adjust to all this extra attention from you—doesn't wind up killing you? The answers come in the form of a careful and unique approach that includes technical advice and emotional balance.

Signs and Symptoms for Self-Diagnosis

Fortunately, this book provides both the technical *and* emotional advice for all four phases of the Entrepreneurial Lifecycle. Unfortunately, it's often difficult to know exactly which phase you and your business are in. There's not exactly a horn that goes off to tell you when you've graduated to the next phase.

For this reason, I have structured this book in a way that allows you to self-diagnose your business. Each chapter presents a phenomenon commonly associated with a specific phase in the Lifecycle. At the start of each chapter, you will find a list of stakeholders, emotions, and common symptoms that you and your stakeholders are likely to experience during this phase. Remember, this is a general guide and *not* an exact science. But based on our experiences working with successful entrepreneurs, we have found that knowing these stakeholders, emotions, and symptoms will help you diagnose what phase your business is in, which will in turn allow you to deploy the best technical and emotional advice for your unique business journey.

Typically, the symptoms of the Lifecycle's phases revolve around the emotions you'll be experiencing most frequently. Sometimes, those emotions are unique to each phase. But in writing this book, I had a revelation: certain emotional conditions like fear, anxiety, and insecurity exist in every phase. They are "recycled." These feelings become that ringing in your ear or that nagging back pain; they're always there, but you learn to live with them. And some days, it's worse than others.

What is interesting is that the triggers for these emotions change, and more importantly, successful individual(s) learn to deal with these triggers and compartmentalize them so the emotions don't consume them. Those who can't master this compartmentalization (or emotional self-control) wind up with a "negative emotional infection," where the feeling spreads to other areas that have no relationship to the negative trigger. Common side effects of this kind of infection include legal actions, defection of a trusted employee, loss of a good client, or termination of the entrepreneurial journey.

Learn to Compartmentalize

Years ago, Waldron Private Wealth was sued for over $1 million by a departing employee. We viewed the suit as an assault on our integrity. The claims were clearly frivolous, and the former employee's attack strategy was an attempt to smear our reputation and to extract a settlement rather than endure the litigation process. On principal, there was no way we would settle. It was difficult at times not to have this obvious emotional trigger negatively impact everything else that was so positive in the firm. It took two years of compartmentalization before the case went to a jury trial. We won and were vindicated, but without the discipline to objectively assess the situation, I might have experienced how anger can hijack a person's thinking.

Good leaders learn to compartmentalize early. If you don't, you could be eaten alive by your own emotions. Plus, there are the health risks. We've all heard stories of nervous breakdowns or heart attacks and other significant health-related problems. This is why diagnosing where you are on the Lifecycle is so important: We're trying to avoid major medical issues as much as we're trying to avoid decisions that could hinder the business.

Having the information you need to diagnose where you are on the Entrepreneurial Lifecycle will allow you to:

- Identify and more effectively address the problems and emotions you're currently experiencing
- Benefit from the experience of other successful business owners and entrepreneurs who have gone through these transitions
- Prepare you and your business for everything you are likely to face as you move toward the next phase

- Communicate more effectively with your family and other stakeholders
- Make your business more efficient so you can free up your time and energy
- Preserve more of the wealth that your business generates
- Guide you through the optimal rate of growth for your unique business
- Prepare you (both emotionally and technically) for the eventual sale or succession of your business
- Lead a more fulfilling life while you are running your business, and after

Sailing through the Lifecycle

Every business is unique, and so is every entrepreneur, but at the same time, we all share a few commonalities. Imagine that your business is a ship sailing across the ocean and that you are its captain. No matter how seasoned you are as a captain or how large, sturdy, and fast your ship happens to be, you're going to face the same elements as anyone else who ventures across the ocean.

Hopefully you don't get seasick, because this journey will be unsteady—you will have challenges and setbacks. There will be strong winds and currents, and sometimes, your crew and passengers will seem like more than you can handle. The stories and lessons contained in this book will help you identify where you are in the journey and what you can expect along the way. This way, you can be *self-aware* about where you are on the journey, you can prepare for any limbic storms that could potentially commandeer your emotions, and you can maintain your self-control so that you can continue on the journey as smoothly as possible.

Three key factors will determine whether you reach your destination: the other people on the ship, the currents, and the wind. Let's briefly address each one.

THE OTHER PEOPLE ON THE SHIP

When you picture your business as a ship making this voyage, do you imagine yourself alone at the wheel? It's fine if you did—many businesses start out this way. A person (or sometimes a partnership or group) starts with a concept, and ideally, that concept grows into something profitable. But a growing company will need more people to help it continue to grow. Your business might start out as a sunfish, but eventually, the business grows into a Royal Clipper that's impossible for a single person to keep under control.

Along the way, you will have to take on a crew to help you manage all the complexities of your ship. This crew includes the people you count on to make your business function. They follow your guidance as captain, manage the day-to-day mechanics, and have a vested interest in helping you reach your destination.

But the crew is only a portion of the other people on your ship. More than likely, you will also take on passengers. These passengers are the stakeholders in your business who materialize as your partnerships evolve and your family grows. They include your spouse, children, grandchildren, partners and investors, and customers or clients. Like your crew, your passengers have a vested interest in where the ship is going and how it gets there.

It is important to pay attention to the expectations and emotional needs of these people, as any one of them could impact the route you take, for better or worse. A happy crew and contented passengers make for a smoother journey. So, over the course of this book, we're going to explore strategies and insights to manage the expectations and emotions of your team and stakeholders.

THE CURRENTS

Whether they're navigating a ship or running a business, even the best leaders tend to overlook the currents. This is because, unlike most of the other factors at play, the currents often show up unannounced, are unseen, and are uncontrollable.

For a business, the currents are the too-often-ignored rate of change and disruption in your industry. Often, the captain can get so focused on the people and the mechanics of his or her ship that the currents pull it off course. This can happen no matter how good a captain is or how strong the ship seems to be. Think about Sears and Kodak, for example. They ignored the currents in their industry and wound up sunk.

This is why, in the chapters to come, I offer a series of technical strategies tailored to each phase of the Entrepreneurial Lifecycle. After you have diagnosed your emotions and symptoms and identified where you stand, these technical strategies will help you reposition your sails to harness the currents of your industry and reach your destination as efficiently as possible.

THE WIND

If you've ever been on a ship, you know that wind direction and speed is easily the most important element to pay attention to from moment to moment. But in business, far too often entrepreneurs fail to demonstrate a mastery of this factor. In our analogy, the wind is the all-encompassing emotional side of entrepreneurship and wealth.

As I have mentioned, the emotional side can be quite complicated. For some of us, these emotions will fire more acutely during certain phases of your business's Lifecycle. Sometimes we can engage with an emotion, master it (or maybe just recognize it), and then be blindsided by its consequences as we move from one phase to the next. For others, certain emotions can be more prevalent in an early phase, disappear for a while, and then show up again when we least expect it.

The winds of fear and anxiety might show up during the Survival Phase as you take on more debt and worry about losing it all. Then, during the Maturation Phase, you might experience a different kind of fear and anxiety as more people start relying on your business for income, and you have to think about things like retooling and expanding into different markets for the first time or considering asset protection. During the Transition Phase, your fear and anxiety revolves around the idea that you might soon have to give up control to someone else. And during the Day After, your fear and anxiety is all about figuring out how to fill those suddenly empty spaces in your life.

These emotions may not seem particularly damaging at first, but if you don't pay attention to them, like the winds they can quickly blow you off course. Conviction, for example, is a continuous belief in yourself and in your plan as you encounter obstacles along the way toward your goal. The best entrepreneurs we have worked with always continue to take action and make decisions and take full responsibility for these actions and decisions when things go wrong. They also learn how to filter through all the unsolicited advice from family, friends, and well-meaning colleagues. They understand that it's important to keep your conviction and self-confidence high without taking it too far.

Trust is similar. Entrepreneurs have to believe in themselves or they won't succeed. But at the same time, they have to be able to trust others (partners, management, vendors, executives, team members, outside professionals, and so on) to help them achieve their goals. At some point, you must learn the ability to delegate. Otherwise, you risk stifling the growth of the company and of your key employees.

And there will always be the winds of luck. Luck, as they say, is where hard work and opportunity meet. It is about getting outside your comfort zone and living on the edge of risk. When you do this, good things tend to happen. But there are also inflection points of luck—don't confuse it with brilliance. Celebrate it, because it happens to every successful entrepreneur. The line to walk is to know how to capitalize on it while also remaining humble. A little naiveté helps as well. A good friend and client of ours once said that law school trained him to identify every risk possible, which was something he later had to *overcome* in his entrepreneurial life. Sometimes, not knowing every risk out there is a good thing. It's great to be a genius, but a little dumb luck can be quite helpful.

The list of people, industry factors, and emotions that can impact your journey is a long one, but as we will see, the key to managing your business is to diagnose your phase of the Entrepreneurial Lifecycle and then carefully follow the technical strategies and emotional lessons that apply to your unique situation. Of course, it also helps to examine some illuminating stories of the successes and setbacks of other entrepreneurs who braved the journey before you. Leveraging their hindsight will help you navigate the wind and current you will encounter as you guide your business through your journey. Let's raise our sails and begin.

PHASE ONE

Survival

CHAPTER ONE

Cash, Debt, and Drive

Stakeholders:

- You
- Your spouse
- Your children (the next generation is an evolving and complex group of stakeholders)
- Your partners (silent or otherwise)
- The bank

Emotions:

- Excitement
- Fear
- Doubt
- Anxiety
- Euphoria
- Motivation/drive
- Trust

Symptoms:

- ✅ Frequent sleepless nights
- ✅ Survival instinct drives you
- ✅ An uneasy feeling from operating outside your comfort zone
- ✅ Emergence of skills you didn't even know you had
- ✅ Small wins feel like enormous validations of your vision
- ✅ Motivation to prove your doubters wrong
- ✅ In some circumstances, risk feels like more than you can bear
- ✅ In other circumstances, risk generates an adrenaline rush

There Are Many Paths to Entrepreneurship

WHETHER YOU'RE JUST STARTING out in business or you're well on your way through its Lifecycle, you probably have some pretty strong feelings about the early days. When I look back, I remember quite a bit of stress following my decision to set out on my own. On the one hand, there was the excitement and conviction. Part of me just *knew* that this venture was going to work. But on the other hand, there was uncertainty, insecurity, and doubt. After all, like many entrepreneurs just starting out, during the Survival Phase, it was only *me*. Apart from my wife, Maureen, I didn't have anyone else to help me overcome the obstacles, so I had to constantly battle with uncertainty during all the early challenges and failures. I did a lot of talking to myself and to Maureen.

Everybody comes to entrepreneurship differently. Some people are born with the drive and freedom to take this kind of leap—and anyway, they couldn't imagine ever having to work for somebody else. They might not have always known what they were going to do, but they have always known that one day they would build something on their own.

Then there are the people who join their family business when it has already reached one of the middle phases of the Lifecycle. Many of them have grown up around this business and have always assumed it would be their role to lead it one day. They may or may not be natural-born entrepreneurs, but they have certainly grown up knowing that one day they would become an entrepreneur.

Finally, there is the longer, more circuitous road to entrepreneurship, where a person tries different careers, learns different skills, spots an opportunity, and then finds their way to that entrepreneurial path. For most people in this camp, a singular event or moment triggers this change in their mindset. One day, they're a career person. Then they encounter an opportunity, and suddenly they're an entrepreneur.

For one client of mine, that opportunity came when he found himself entangled in union politics. Dan is a charismatic, natural-born leader. As a young man, he was popular among the rank and file union workers in his city. This popularity threatened the union president so much that he had Dan blackballed from any job within a hundred miles. This made life very hard for Dan, a young husband and father of three. One night, following a contentious meeting at his union hall, Dan found himself in an elevator with three large gentlemen who disagreed with his point of view. Back in the early '70s, union tensions were high—high enough that these three large gentlemen forced the elevator to stop and then tried to beat Dan's opinion out of him. They hadn't counted on their opponent being a tenacious former Marine. After the encounter, Dan restarted the elevator, reached the ground floor, stepped over his three opponents, and exited the elevator.

During the brawl, he lost a couple of teeth that he didn't find until the next morning after two cups of coffee (or as he puts it, those teeth really came back to "bite me in the ass"). More importantly, that encounter on the elevator convinced Dan that the time had come to leave the union for a safer job running his own equipment rental business. Hopefully your own wake-up call, if you've had one, wasn't as painful. And hopefully you will meet with every bit as much success as Dan, who went on to grow that company over a period of forty years before selling it for over $300 million.

Another client happened upon an entrepreneurial opportunity when a good friend of his died in a surfing accident. The friend had started developing technology that his estate didn't know what to do with, so my client offered to buy the rights to implement this technology. He already owned another business, but he decided that the time was right to become a serial entrepreneur (more on this topic later), and *boom*, he started another business and hit the ground running.

Each of these entrepreneurs achieved their success in part because of their willingness to take risks. The more risk you take, the higher the potential for success (or failure). You get outside your comfort zone, and then you work harder and dig deeper than you ever thought possible. Hopefully, in the end, you succeed.

If you're in the Survival Phase, chances are you have found your opportunity and you are skilled in ways that will help you meet that opportunity. Here is where we start looking for the technical strategies and emotional insights that will not only help you weather the dangerous Survival Phase but will guide you to a level of achievement similar to those wildly successful clients who bravely took the leap.

Mixed Emotions in the Survival Phase

The term "survival" comes from the notion that you're mostly just clawing and scratching to keep your business alive. And the struggle is real. According to a study by Harvard Business School senior lecturer Shikhar Ghosh, 75 percent of venture-backed start-ups fail.[5] Also, according to the Small Business Association, 30 percent of all new businesses fail during the first two years, 50 percent during the first five years, and 66 percent during the first ten years.[6]

---

5   Faisal Hoque, "Why Most Venture-Backed Companies Fail," *Fast Company*, December 12, 2010, https://www. fastcompany.com/3003827/why-most-venture-backed-companies-fail.
6   U.S. Department of Commerce, Census Bureau, Business Dynamics Statistics; U.S. Department of Labor, Bureau of Labor Statistics, BED.

Numbers like these can be terrifying, of course, but let's consider the positives about the Survival Phase. For instance, in some ways, running your business is as simple as it is ever going to be. Yes, the financial and technical stresses are high, but the number of stakeholders is the lowest it is ever going to be. The more your business grows, the more stakeholders you will take on, and the more people you will have to satisfy.

Right now, it's just you, your family, and your partners (if you have them). Even if the money always seems tight and the day-to-day stresses are high, try to take comfort in the knowledge that you have a comparatively small number of people to keep happy. Meanwhile, your lifestyle is less complicated and less expensive now than it will be after your business meets with success, and you currently have fewer complexities to manage.

Obviously, it's easier to state these truths than it is to believe them—especially when you're living them in the moment. Entrepreneurs in this phase will have sleepless nights, stress, and anxiety. But it's important to try to enjoy the fact that this portion of the Lifecycle presents you with so many opportunities to discover what you can do. New strengths and skills you didn't even know you had will start to emerge as the excitement and demands of building a business moves you out of your comfort zone. You might, for instance, find yourself tapping into some previously unrealized people skills, management skills, and even sales skills. After all, if you're going to keep your creditors at bay, then you have no choice but to make sales. It's that famous Thomas J. Watson quote, "Nothing happens in business until something gets sold."

Now that I've boosted your spirits, let's return to everyone's favorite subject and talk about creditors. It's true that most entrepreneurs in the early days of the Entrepreneurial Lifecycle are absolutely *swimming* in debt. This can make every day feel like a fight for your life. Many entrepreneurs have to take out second mortgages, solicit financial help from family and friends, or fall under the thumb of outside investors. In this way, creditors become other stakeholders in your business. These circumstances tend to engender feelings of helplessness—the sense that much of what you're trying to do is beyond your control, because if just one thing goes wrong or is delayed, you'll drown in a sea of debt.

The funny thing about these warring emotions of excitement, anxiety, and fear is that while they can certainly cripple you with doubt, they can also motivate and inspire. It all depends on how you are hardwired to react. Young businesses come with a host of unique challenges, but your conflicted emotions motivate you to meet those challenges with at least something resembling confidence that you will succeed. One of the more positive side effects of this phenomenon is that whenever you *do* succeed, those small wins can make you feel like you're on top of the world and nothing can stop you. The negative side effect, however, is that euphoria and overconfidence can compel you to make rash choices that end up harming your business.

For anyone in your shoes, the energy related to doing something new, exhilarating, creative, and self-driven mixes with all that fear and debt-related desperation to create a potent emotional cocktail—one that is sure to keep you up at night. So while we will explore some technical strategies to consider as you move your business toward the Growth Phase, the more immediate need to address is how to channel the emotional side. Finding that balance starts with examining the source of the emotions at play. No matter what kind of business you run or who your stakeholders happen to be, the source of your emotions is likely one or more of the same three factors: debt, cash flow, and drive.

Failures Will Happen: Embrace Them

Before we go any further, let's get an important point clear: Failure will happen. This is just another one of those ubiquitous conditions in all the entrepreneurial situations that we have had the privilege of assisting clients with at Waldron Private Wealth. Once you accept that failure will happen, the key is to embrace it, learn from it, and hopefully use the lesson so that the failure doesn't become fatal for your business.

Then again, sometimes failure *is* fatal to the entrepreneurial venture. Notice that I wrote "fatal to the entrepreneurial venture" and not "fatal to the entrepreneur." Most entrepreneurs are like salmon swimming upstream; they can easily be taken out by the many outside forces and risks that they can't control. For the salmon, it is the bear or the fly-fisher; for the entrepreneur, it is the economy, market conditions, regulatory change, disruption, stakeholder challenges, and of course, emotional paralysis or implosion. Failures are sometimes fatal to the venture, but it is important that they don't also become fatal to the entrepreneurs.

A client of ours named Carl is living proof of this lesson, as his entrepreneurial spirit compelled him to start two companies that both ended in failure. Yes, these companies died, but Carl himself wasn't dead. So he started yet a third business, and this one has grown into a fantastic, wildly successful, and highly valuable company. Carl had the insight to recognize that failure will happen, and he learned from those failures. He applied this knowledge to ensure that the third time around would be the charm.

If you prefer high-profile examples, then think about Steve Jobs after he was forced out of Apple. He probably wasn't too wild about finding himself removed from the company he'd helped create. When something like that happens to most people, it can spur spite, resentment, or any number of other damaging feelings. But that's part of what made Jobs one of the most celebrated entrepreneurs of his time. He took that moment and harnessed it—he used it as *motivation* to succeed in ways even grander than before. The result: He made the leap to Pixar, built it into an entertainment juggernaut, and eventually leveraged the opportunity to return to Apple and grow it into the technological and cultural behemoth it is today.

If tech isn't your thing, think of Adolf and Rudolf Dassler, two brothers who used a sibling disagreement to found Adidas and Puma, respectively, two of the world's largest and most successful sports apparel companies. At first glance, it might seem as if it was spite or a desire for revenge that drove these men to prove their doubters wrong and reach great heights. But the truth is actually the opposite. These leaders leaned not on their spite, but on their *inner drive* to find success.

As the stories of Carl, Steve Jobs, Adolf and Rudolf Dassler, and others show us, it's not whether we'll face tough times; it's about how we *react* to them. The reaction is one of those factors that separates dreamers from true entrepreneurs. For the latter camp, setbacks ignite a fire to prove one's doubters and detractors wrong. (In my experience, the most important person they want to prove success to is themselves.) It is a phenomenon that strengthens your conviction in what you're trying to do with your business, sustains you during those sleepless nights, and makes you endure all those troubling times when it looks like this endeavor might not be working.

Debt Can Be a Great Motivator

Before I started Waldron Private Wealth, I worked for a "Big Eight" accounting firm.[7] Then one day, like so many entrepreneurs before and after me, I had an epiphany. One moment, I was a CPA with a steady income, health insurance, and other benefits, and the next, I felt inspired to start my own business.

---

7   During the 1970s and '80s, there were eight large multinational accounting firms, referred to as the "Big Eight."

I'll never forget the experience that led to my epiphany. A prospective client had come into the office to hear my recommendations on his financial situation, and I suggested that he should take a $4 million distribution from his C-Corporation for tax purposes, invest those funds in the appropriate allocation, recapitalize his company to an LLC with voting and nonvoting shares, and transfer the nonvoting shares to a trust.

The prospect was thrilled about the comprehensiveness of the strategy. He made it clear that he wasn't used to such a coordinated plan and that he looked forward to working with one person on these matters instead of having to consult with a collection of financial professionals from different companies to execute the strategy. "You're hired," he said. "Go ahead and get it done."

"I can't," I said. The truth was that we could manage *some* of these steps at the accounting firm that employed me, but the rest of them (due to a variety of regulatory restrictions) we couldn't. I was facing industry impediments to serving my clients in the way I envisioned they needed to be served. "The AICPA [American Institute of Certified Public Accountants] prohibits us from getting involved in the execution of securities transactions," I explained.

The prospect took a good, long look at me. "Well, then what good are you?" he asked.

That was my aha moment. I realized that I had to leave public accounting so I could provide the comprehensive, integrated strategies that so many business leaders and families of wealth demand. Six months later, I left public accounting and founded what would become Waldron Private Wealth.

When I started, I had a vision of a comprehensive, fiduciary service model that was quite different than other financial services firms, and which would meet a strong demand from business owners and wealthy individuals and families. This would be an independent wealth management firm that understood the interrelated effects of income tax, estate planning, investment management, cash flow, risk management, business succession planning, philanthropy, debt, and the other components that make up a client's financial life—a firm that could devise a comprehensive approach to timely identification of risk and opportunity, the evaluation of solutions and strategies, and executing those solutions and strategies with the client's other professional team members, such as accountants and attorneys.

The firm would have three founding principles:

1. Develop an investment management offering free from the conflicts of interest that come with trading stocks, bonds, mutual funds, and other financial products on commission.
2. Add professionals to the team who have a wide array of expertise.
3. Be selective of the clients we serve, and don't try to be all things to all people (at the time of this writing, we work with approximately 180 families). We focus on providing customized services to individuals, families, and family offices who struggle with the stress and complexity that come from increasing wealth. This is a deeply personal task. Therefore we keep our employee-to-client ratio to 5:1. Competitors often have that in excess of 100:1. (That is when you feel like a number.)

Sitting here today, it is clear that I was onto something. I am proud of our firm, which has been recognized by peers, clients, and national media as an industry leader. We have a great team and great clients. However, the road to success was hard, to say the least.

I'm a planner by nature, so of course I had a great plan in place before I took the leap. First, I decided to quit my job only days after Maureen and I were approved for a mortgage on our first house. I knew that I would never get the mortgage if I couldn't show current employment income on my application, so I purchased the house (and acquired the debt) without the security of a steady paycheck.

Still, I wasn't worried, because I had spent some time lining up four clients who were willing to engage me for my unique service offering and provide me with a smooth economic transition. As one of the best entrepreneurs I have ever worked with later told me, "The most important thing to have when you start your business is a customer." And I had *four* of them. As far as I was concerned, everything would be smooth sailing because I could always count on the revenue from those four initial clients to help me establish and grow my business. Ah, to be thirty years old again. When we're that young and naive (especially as entrepreneurs), we don't even know how good we have it.

You can see where this is going: None of the four clients followed through (at least initially). I quickly learned that John Waldron, new business owner, was seen in a very different light than John Waldron, employee of Deloitte. Imagine that! So there I was, thirty years old, jobless, up to my eyeballs in new debt, and with no revenue coming in. I had some savings accumulated from my accounting career that I could lean on, but in the meantime, the runway was terrifyingly short.

It was so short, in fact, that it filled me with doubt. Only a few weeks after setting off on my own, I called a recruiter to see if I could get a salaried job with another Big Eight accounting firm. Fortunately, the headhunter wasn't in (lucky break #1) and I had to leave a message. Before she returned my call, I wound up meeting my first client (lucky break #2). When the recruiter called back, I told her I would get back to her. Hopefully, she isn't still waiting.

And then, before long, an old acquaintance asked for my help on a project. From that project sprang other relationships and opportunities. Eventually, two of those four initial clients finally did take the leap (once it was clear that I had found solid ground). And suddenly, I had a fully functional business. It turned out that the idea that had driven me to leave public accounting in the first place was a good one. This philosophy of helping people deal with the increasing complexities that come with increasing wealth appealed to my target audience, and more importantly, it *worked*.

Of course, in hindsight it's easier to focus on the positive outcome. For the long weeks and months between first setting up shop and running into that first real opportunity, debt was a great motivator for me, but also a painful one. In a lot of ways, as I will elaborate on in the next chapter, it was also a blessing because it forced me to change my mindset. Before my debts started bearing down, I'd thought that I was strictly a CPA. But then circumstance forced me to be a *salesman* as well. Being a salesman meant refining my value proposition in a very crowded field. (In our business, we compete with brokers and investment banks who claim to do the same.) And that deep, introspective dive into my value proposition forced me to clearly articulate it to myself, which I could then easily share with prospects, and later, to my team.

That's the power of debt: It motivates you to do things you used to think impossible. It forces you to get outside your comfort zone. So yes, in the Survival Phase, you're bound to lose a lot of sleep. But the positive side of not sleeping is that it gives you plenty of time to figure out how to push your own abilities to the limit, expand your capabilities, and do what needs to be done. You will develop a keen sense of *self-awareness* to understand the stress-triggers within you, and *self-control* to extinguish the negative energy and turn that stress into positive momentum. If you don't develop this self-awareness and self-control, prepare to be eaten alive.

Making Payroll in the Pool Hall

I started my business on what felt like an overwhelming amount of debt, but it was nothing compared to a client of mine who we'll call Russ. This client had his aha moment back when he was a welder and someone asked him if he could install an alarm system in his house. Russ had no experience with anything related to alarm systems, but he figured out how to wire the house and connect the system to a monitoring service that could rapidly deploy a police response.

The project was such a success that Russ quit his welding job and took out a $50,000 loan on his house, which at the time was an even more staggering amount than it sounds like today. Like so many entrepreneurs, Russ wore a lot of hats. Every aspect of the business flowed through him. But when it came time to take on other people to help his new business meet the rapidly growing demand for the service, he knew he had to find a way.

Russ learned that, even in a business with what feels like a fair amount of revenue, cash flow is like picking up water: It runs through your fingers. The more revenue you bring in, the more you grow, and the more you grow, the more expenses you have and the more you need to invest. You never do fully grasp cash; you just find ways to manage the flow and grow as comfortably as possible.

Payday at Russ's company was always on Wednesdays. Most of the time, he would barely be able to cover the payroll. But sometimes, he could see that he was going to come up a little short. For most business owners, the solution in these situations is first to see if you can expand your credit. Next, it's to visit everyone you know with your hand out. Sometimes it can feel a little like the playground when you were a kid, when all your friends turned their pockets inside out and threw everything they had into the pot. But there came a point in Russ's early journey as an entrepreneur where he had already exhausted those resources. So he got resourceful. Whenever he was short on pay, he would go down to the local pool hall and hustle until he'd won enough to make payroll.

We're not all as skilled with a pool cue as Russ, but his lesson rings true no matter what your business or abilities. In a setting where cash flow is king, sometimes you have to get creative. Sometimes you have to be more resourceful than you ever realized you could be. It's a little like getting a campfire going. If it's a life or death situation, even when you don't have any matches, you don't give up; you look for rocks to strike together to create a spark. Russ found his spark in the pool hall. And he grew his business to be one of the largest home security firms in the country.

Emotional Lessons:

- Most of the entrepreneurs we have worked with will tell you that the positive and negative feelings associated with Survival are often at war. Getting them all to work together—getting your inspiration to mesh with your drive and your motivation to eliminate your doubt— is something of a balancing act.

- It might seem like the emotional side of the picture couldn't get more complicated than it is right now, but running a new business is like having a newborn. When you have a newborn (particularly if we're talking about your first child), the emotions can be extreme. Everything you have to do each day seems so complicated. But then, as your newborn grows, each new year brings on even more complexities. At some point, you look back and wonder why you ever thought the newborn phase was challenging to begin with, because children, as they grow up and morph into teenagers, can be so much more complicated to manage.

  The same is true of a business. Each new phase brings new complexities. For now, your emotions will feel extreme and the choices you have to make will seem overwhelmingly complicated. But that's only because you're in survival mode. It's literally live or die here. In some ways, that raises the stakes. But in others, it makes the emotional side *less* difficult to manage. Remember that everything you're feeling and everything you must do contributes to one thing: survival. Simply survive. That's all you have to do.

- Don't let your fear and anxiety consume you, or it may dissolve your passion, destroy your ability to impart that same passion to people around you, and worst of all, ruin your health.

- On the other end of the spectrum, it's important to keep a pragmatic view. This is my favorite piece of advice for entrepreneurs in the Survival Phase, because I went through it myself and had to learn it the hard way. Sometimes you're going to win. But when that happens, don't fall into the trap of assuming that it's because you're some kind of infallible genius. Sometimes wins are just a matter of luck. "Don't get too high on the highs or too low on the lows," as I like to say.

- Embrace your mistakes and failures; they are inevitable, so learn from them.

- Be aware of when goals and stakeholders change for you and your partners. These factors can alter the motivational and emotional components of your business. The more you know about your stakeholders and what they expect of the business, the easier it will be to balance their emotions (and yours), and the smoother your journey into the Maturation Phase will be.

Technical Strategies:

- In the Survival Phase, the technical strategies to keep in line are the most basic of all: your cash flow, your capital, and your corporate and ownership structure. You must also stay current with all your regulatory filings and licenses.

- Be sure to incorporate properly and shield any assets you have from potential creditors. It helps to find a good corporate attorney and CPA so that all your filings and basic contracts are strong.

- For any business starting out with outside professional money or venture capital, it is important to have a thorough understanding of your capital structure, valuation, and control triggers.

- If you are going it alone with no partners, then let's face it, during the Survival Phase, you're going to be spending too much time running around and putting out fires to worry about a host of technical and tax strategies. At this point, unless you are starting out with venture money, the main technical matter to keep in mind is your cash inflow vs. cash outflow ratio. Cash flow is the lifeblood of any business, but it's particularly true of businesses in this phase.

- If you've seen genuine potential in this business, and it looks like it's just a matter of keeping your cash flow ahead of your debt for a short while, then find cash anywhere you can. Pledge every asset you have to get lines of credit. Raid savings and retirement accounts if you have to. Raid the couch cushions.

- Now if you're in the process of buying an existing business, there's more complexity. Unless you're lucky enough to have a huge bankroll going in, cash flow will always be a problem early on. You'll start with what feels like plenty of resources, but those resources will extend to their breaking point quicker than you can believe. Cash and resource management are extremely critical in this phase.

Be Collaborative, Entrepreneurial, and Driven

Of all the qualities of the successful entrepreneurs I have had the privilege of working with over the years, one of the most important and unanimously present abilities is to share your passion and conviction with other people. For our most successful clients, the ability comes quite easily and naturally. This is because the leadership trait is based on their commitment and responsibility to their employees.

From this genuine trait emerges one of the most critical emotional elements required for the success of your organization: trust. If they trust you and your commitment to them, and if they trust your convic-tion to the mission, then you will ignite their entrepreneurial spirit, and you will get their best effort and ideas. If you can pull this off, then it serves as the initial formation and the basis for your company's culture. Today, the cultural mission at Waldron Private Wealth is to be collabo-rative, entrepreneurial, and driven to make a difference for our clients, colleagues, and our team members—and it all stems from trust.

CHAPTER TWO

Where Does the Money Come From?

Stakeholders:

- You
- Your spouse
- Your children
- Your partner(s)
- Your investor(s) or banker(s)

Emotions:

- Fear
- Anxiety
- Insecurity
- Trust
- Pride
- Embarrassment
- Loneliness
- Desperation

Symptoms:

- ✔ Obsessive focus on money
- ✔ Heightened sense of urgency
- ✔ Fear-induced creative drive
- ✔ Desire to satisfy your investors
- ✔ Awkwardness at the Thanksgiving dinner table
- ✔ Looking for signs of traction and small wins for proof of concept
- ✔ Fear of loss of flexibility (either in terms of finances or freedom to pursue opportunities)

THROUGHOUT THE SURVIVAL PHASE, you're going to be thinking an awful lot about money. It's what moves the product or service lines, keeps the lights on, pays the rent, and ensures that your employees get paid. And then hopefully there's enough left over to put food on your table. For any young business, adequate start-up capital is essential. Unfortunately, most aren't adequately capitalized at the beginning. This is why it's strange that so many entrepreneurs never bother identifying the emotional and technical strings attached to a fundamentally important question: Where is the money coming from?

The Four Sources

No two businesses are exactly alike, but all businesses in their early stages get their capital from four sources (often, it's a combination of the four). Each source comes with different challenges and risks, different technical strategies, and just as importantly, a different set of emotional challenges. Knowing the specific risks, strategies, and emotions that apply to your unique capital situation is a huge part of the battle to advance to the Maturation Phase.

SELF-FINANCING

This is where you pool your own money and assets together to fund your business. You raid your retirement and savings accounts to fund your business and personal life. At this stage, the line between business and personal isn't just blurred; the line *doesn't exist*.

BANK FINANCING

You receive a loan from a bank that you use either to start your business or supplement its capital structure. You leverage your house, your kids, your cat, your dog, you max out personal and business credit cards, and you intimately learn the concept of "float."

ANGEL INVESTORS

This source is otherwise known as "friends and family," or more crassly as "unsophisticated money." It goes by these terms because the funding typically comes from friends, family, or others who contribute capital to your business not because they're trying to invest professionally, but because they have a personal and emotional connection with you and do not have the heart to say no, or they believe in you and want to help get your company off the ground.

Many of our clients are frequently asked to serve as this kind of investor for someone else in their lives. This is a true test to see which part of the brain makes the decision: the emotional side or the logical, rational-thinking side. More on this later, because if you are lucky enough to survive this stage into the Maturation Phase, family and friends will start coming to *you* for money, and you will confront this dilemma from the other side.

VENTURE CAPITAL AND PRIVATE EQUITY: PROFESSIONAL MONEY

VENTURE CAPITAL (VC) VERSUS PRIVATE EQUITY (PE)

THESE ARE TWO ALTERNATIVE sources of capital for private companies that have similar characteristics and a few differences. They key similarities are—

1. They invest in private companies with high potential that the investors believe will deliver above average returns.

2. They can assist these companies with technology and management in addition to access to capital.

3. They typically look to exit their investment within five to seven years.

The key difference between VC and PE is that VCs typically invest in start-ups in the survival stage of their journey while PEs invest in companies that are likely in their maturation phase.

For purposes of this discussion, I refer to both as "professional money."

With professional money, the arrangement typically involves giving up a portion of your current and future equity to a professional investment group in exchange for the capital, professional insight, and other resources your business needs today. When and how to optimize the usage of professional money is a separate book in itself. Suffice to say that this can be by far the most expensive method of capitalizing your company because you undoubtedly will be giving up more potential future upside. This is expensive if you are successful. But if you are *not* successful, then this is likely the cheapest way to raise capital without straining relationships with friends and family. Then again, no one starts a business thinking they're going to fail.

The other consistent observation about professional money is that there is a completely different emotional attachment. When the money comes from a faceless group of investors represented by a "suit," you tend to form a comparatively unemotional, impersonal relationship with your capital. It is a transactional relationship, unlike the relationship you enjoy with your spouse, your friends and family, and even your house. Just this week, I had a glass of wine with a friend and client who described how the company he now controls was previously owned by a scientist who had invented a great technology.[8] The company had received $100 million of VC funding, and they blew through it all with a $20 million per month burn rate. And they describe venture capital as "smart money"! This of course created the opportunity for my friend to take control of the company at a great valuation given the value assigned to his operational, turnaround, and management experience.

Depending on which source(s) of capital your business relies upon, you're going to be dealing with many different factors and new stakeholders on the emotional and technical spectrum. The emotions can feel more personal and urgent for some sources (like family and friends) and less so for others (like professional money). Typically, the tradeoff is that you're offering more control and equity upside for the chance to sleep a little better at night knowing that it's less of your own money or your family's or friends' money at risk. At the same time, the reward you can expect for your ultimate success varies greatly depending on where you're getting your capital. It's like everything in business: The more risk you assume, the greater reward you can achieve.

The funny thing is that even though they worry about money constantly during the Survival Phase, many entrepreneurs don't stop to

---

8   These types have the worst track records as entrepreneurs, by the way.

think about how different sources require different strategies. Instead, they scrape together their technical strategies day by day, which causes them to feel emotionally drained by their capital-related challenges. This time-honored "flying by the seat of your pants" approach works for some—particularly if you're a born entrepreneur—but it's also a big part of why 70 percent of all new businesses fail. So let's avoid any pants-related flying by getting to know the specific rigors of each source and then figuring out how to adjust your technical and rewards expectations accordingly.

Different Entrepreneurs, Different Risk Tolerance

One factor that may have leapt out at you about those four potential sources for funding is that they all feature different levels of risk. Where you reside on the spectrum of funding depends quite a bit on your circumstances, but also on your risk tolerance. This week I called one of my longest tenured clients to ask him about the subject. Charles sold his technology business in 1996. "Luck has more to it than risk-taking," he said. "I didn't take much risk in my business. I didn't go into a lot of debt or take outside money because tech isn't capital asset intensive. Luck had more to do with it." This point really struck me, as it shows that everyone views and values risk differently.

Early on in my Survival Phase, I was at the peak leverage point before significant traction occurred. As I faced that leverage point, I started to get a little more risk-averse. That was when I spoke to a colleague about becoming a partner in my business. With a wife, three young children at home, and a sizeable mortgage, I found myself so attracted to the concept of risk reduction, and so overcome by the feeling of insecurity and the pressure of debt, that my emotions drowned out the voice in my head that said, *This is the worst idea ever.* The craziest part is that it didn't even make sense on paper.

Fortunately, my prospective partner calculated his risk according to the lost opportunity of his salary, stock options, and other intangible career-loss costs. Ultimately, he decided that the risk was too great, and he wound up passing. Fortunately, like the unanswered call to the recruiter, I can count that partnership not working out as a *lucky* moment for me.

Whatever your risk tolerance, the most important lesson to take away from these stories is that confidence is important. Calculate your tolerance for risk, and then plow forward in your venture and don't give that calculation a second thought!

Required: Capital Adequacy

For many years, my three sons and I have enjoyed scuba diving. The hobby has one overriding basic principle: Do not run out of air. If you do, you die. In business, money is air. If you run out of money, you die. Despite this clear correlation, most start-ups don't adequately anticipate and provide for their capital needs. I don't know the exact percentages, but in my experience, and that of my business, this is one of the most common reasons for start-up failure. It accounts for much of the failure that happens during the Maturation Phase as well.

Not anticipating capital needs has a compounding effect: raising money requires a lot of time and effort to be taken away from the core business; when your business is in a vulnerable state, that fact becomes obvious to potential investors (this shifts negotiation leverage, which in turn makes it very expensive, and potentially even impossible, to raise additional capital); and all of those emotions of anxiety, fear, paranoia, and insecurity are at their extremes. The first two effects are obviously detrimental to any company, but don't underestimate that last point either. I have seen emotional extremes cause meltdowns, breakdowns, and breakups of partnerships and marriages.

So, like with scuba diving, always know your oxygen levels. And keep in mind that we're looking for *adequate* capital, not simply *lots of capital*. As I mentioned in the VC example, too much capital isn't good either. What is the right amount of capital? That is the million-dollar question, and it's unique to every venture. Let's examine a few scenarios to see which applies best to yours.

Self-Financing: A Matter of Comfort and Pride

If you can find ways to manage your fear and anxiety, then there are significant advantages to running your business with your own finances. For one, this approach usually means that you have *less* capital to work with than you would have had by taking on an outside investor. With less capital, entrepreneurs tend to get more creative. The far more detrimental outcome attached to failure also leads to a heightened sense of urgency to succeed. This compels the entrepreneur to get outside his or her comfort zone more often—and coincidentally, getting outside your comfort zone is the surest way to keep your business growing. While you're engaged with that growth and getting some traction for the business, the urgency and creativity only builds, because now you have to figure out how to finance this project as it grows. There is something to be said for the survival instinct: It motivates in ways that pressure from outside investors never could.

Then there is pride. Building a business brick by brick is one of the most satisfying achievements I have ever experienced, and I am certainly not alone. Every successful entrepreneur I have worked with says the same thing: Their successful business is one of their greatest sources of pride. It defines who you are and becomes a part of your identity. This is often less true with professional money. After all, the more other people are involved in the financing, the more expectations you have to meet; and the more expectations you have to meet, the less personal the success feels. With professional money, it's no longer day by day, brick by brick; it becomes more like paint by number, where you are following someone else's specific plan.

There is also the financial reward of going it alone. If you manage to start your business exclusively with your own money and then grow it to where it is hugely profitable and eventually saleable, then all that reward goes straight to you and your partners and not to the faceless investors. The path to that point is more challenging, stressful, and personal, but the outcome is substantially more rewarding, both financially and personally.

Bank Financing: Creative Combined Capital Sources

For most entrepreneurs, if they don't have the money and assets to finance the Survival Phase of their business on their own, the first place they turn to is a bank. Some situations lead to favorable terms for the entrepreneur, but more often than not, traditional bank funding is difficult to get. Most modern start-ups don't have much of anything *bankable*. Unless we're talking about an acquisition of a struggling company with bankable assets like a manufacturing plant or piece of real estate to use as collateral, then it's unlikely that a traditional bank is an option. The less tangible nature of technology, healthcare, and other service businesses makes it more difficult to secure a loan with acceptable terms.

Even so, many entrepreneurs find themselves personally guaranteeing small loans, using credit cards, or opening lines of credit to supplement their initial capital that usually comes from depleting their savings. Others may look opportunistically at government-funded programs like the Small Business Administration or funding for minority-owned companies. Because they are usually offered at favorable terms, it is always worth exploring the many grants and capital available to promote new businesses and employment. Over the years, I have seen some amazing financing solutions for some persistent entrepreneurs. Desire, hunger, and necessity tend to drive creative solutions. Just keep in mind that you are working with governmental bodies, which requires tremendous patience.

Other entrepreneurs wind up in situations that we might describe as unconventional bank financing, which includes takeovers, turnarounds, and workouts. In these scenarios, the business is already up and running, oftentimes the bank is already involved, and suddenly the bank has a need to change the terms or leadership structure to get the business back on the right track and salvage their investment. Your entrepreneurial industry or turnaround skills put the negotiation leverage in your hands.

Two entrepreneurs we'll call Paul and Steve got their start in exactly this way, and they're two of the most successful people I know. Paul is a client of Waldron Private Wealth. He and Steve started as employees of a company where they were small equity owners. A bank was already on the hook at the time, and the current owner and leadership group was clearly taking the business in the wrong direction. The threat of defaulting on the bank debt loomed on the horizon. So the bank, through their covenants, stepped into the company, fired management, and made a choice about how to recoup as much of their investment as possible. It would have been easier to exercise their right to liquidate everything, but to this bank, the reward for getting the company back on track was too attractive to pass up.

Ultimately, the bank concluded that they were not equipped to run an international brokerage business. The best opportunity to recover their outstanding loans was to pick stronger leaders from inside the company itself. Enter Paul and Steve, two employees with complementary skill sets that seemed like the perfect mix to turn the company around. The London bank absorbed the equity interest of the original leaders of the company and pledged that equity to Paul and Steve. This was how, practically overnight, these two employees of the business became entrepreneurs with a vested interest and a bank financier. Suddenly they each owned 50 percent of an international money brokerage company.

After Paul and Steve put together the new business plan, the bank agreed to restructure the debt terms without personal guarantees to help clear the path for an increased probability of success. In this way, these two entrepreneurs learned the two key lessons about financing with a bank: It is nice to have the issue of your capital financing behind you so you are clear to focus on the core business issues, particularly when you're still dealing with a matter of survival; and the day after the bank works as your partner (putting you in the ownership position and restructuring the covenants and the *very aggressive* repayment schedule), they will make it abundantly clear that they are looking forward to their quarterly payments. The bank would be Paul and Steve's third partner, at least until the loan was substantially paid off. In any event, the two men found it nice to be in an ownership position with terms that fit within their business plan.

The emotional side of working with a bank is somewhat similar to leveraging your own assets, except that there is less fear about where the money will come from and less anxiety about failure. After all, it's not your money. Yes, to some degree you are on the hook for your capital investment, but ultimately the bank is assuming a sizeable portion of the inherent risk in the venture. Plus, having access to the bank's many products, services, and support staff makes the whole process feel a lot less lonely than when it's just you on the hook.

The credit facility offered to you by the bank removes the stress about how you're going to make payroll or rent next month—after all, these matters are already resolved by the business plan the bank has approved and agreed to fund. This can, in turn, allow you to focus on more pressing needs related to building or turning around the business. If you don't have to think about the rent, you can concentrate more of your time and effort on innovation and creative strategies for growth.

Angel Investors: Unsophisticated, Emotional Money

When I think about angel investing, I often picture an entrepreneur going door-to-door asking for money from his or her family and friends. I see a young, inspired man or woman doing everything possible to scrape together what he or she thinks is enough money to launch a business and create positive cash flow. This is part of why it is sometimes called "unsophisticated money" or "unprofessional money." There's simply not as much financial complexity involved—it's just a dreamer with an idea for a business accepting money from the people who love or believe in him or her and their idea. The terms are usually more favorable for the borrower, but the stress levels related to the prospect of losing this money tend to be higher. With a personal loan, after all, the *results* become more personal. This is why I sometimes call it "emotional money."

At the end of the day, so what if it's called unsophisticated, unprofessional, or emotional? No matter where it comes from, money is money, a loan is a loan, and some of the *most* sophisticated, professional, and successful companies in history have started with angel investing. Back in 1994, Jeff Bezos was a thirty-year-old vice president at a Wall Street hedge fund. That was when he spotted an opportunity: With internet usage growing at 2,300 percent per year, he started brainstorming a business plan that could align with this remarkable growth.[9] He approached his parents with an idea of starting a company that would sell books online—he chose books because of their low cost and high demand. (Remember, this was the '90s; printed books were still widely popular.)

According to Bezos, the majority of the start-up capital for Amazon came from his parents' life savings. They pledged $250,000 of their own money because they believed in their son, even after he told them

---

9 "Amazon Startup Story," Fundable.com, 2018, https://www.fundable.com/learn/startup-stories/amazon.

there was a 70 percent chance that they would lose everything. So the loan itself was slightly less sophisticated, but the results were certainly professional. At the time of this writing, Amazon is one of the world's most valuable companies, and Jeff Bezos is the richest man alive (prior to his divorce).

There's an old saying about angel investing: If it works out, everyone is happy; if not, Thanksgiving dinner gets a little awkward. If you borrow from your family and friends, then your personal financial risk is somewhat lessened (because, after all, it's someone else's money), but the associated anxiety is considerably higher. Since the money often comes from people you love and care about, there's still plenty of pressure to ensure a positive result. In many ways, you enjoy those same benefits of urgency and creativity that come naturally when it's your own money on the line. At the same time, you also enjoy the flexibility that accompanies starting out with a larger investment—particularly when that investment has fewer financial strings attached than a bank or VC loan.

The main problem with angel investing is that while it's nice to get started with outside money, it also often leads to a pattern of consistently needing more. Many entrepreneurs with angel investors find themselves not only in the business of *starting* this company but also in the business of continuously raising money by selling the story to other investors. If you start with only your own money, you have to build brick by brick, and the foundation often turns out stronger. But if you start with a larger sum than you could have afforded on your own, you're able to set your foundation in a hurry, which can make the whole structure a little shakier. In these instances, you may find yourself running around in those early days looking for cash you can use to patch the cracks.

Sometimes you succeed in patching the cracks. Sometimes you don't. I have worked with plenty of entrepreneurs who say that one of their biggest regrets was not raising enough money in the early days. At its worst, this can put the venture at risk of failure with all your angels' investments on the line. At its best, it requires you to invest a great deal of your time and energy to simply raising capital. This can sap you of the bandwidth you need to focus on the other key components of the business. Constantly having to worry about raising money can take away from what your business is supposed to be all about. There are tradeoffs to each path.

Another tradeoff of going with angel investors is that you don't get to enjoy the technical business analysis that you might receive from a professional investor like a bank or a venture capitalist. Instead of professional insight, you could find yourself with the emotional baggage of an unsophisticated investor.

Either way, you will be driven by your sense of pride—a strong desire to avoid failure and to show your investors that they were right to trust you. Your investors will demonstrate that same combination of pride and emotional attachment to the money itself. They're going to be proud of your accomplishments but also fearful of what they stand to lose if you don't come through. The emotional component of this relationship can be small, medium, or large, depending on your relationship with the investor, but the emotional component will always be there. No one wants to sit at the Thanksgiving dinner table under the specter of losing someone else's $250,000. The drive to succeed adjusts accordingly.

Professional Money

Sometimes it can be difficult for young entrepreneurs who are myopically focused on their concept, vision, product, or invention to pay enough attention to the technical side of growing the business. They only see what's in front of them: what they must do today to take that next step toward progress. Often, they realize their concept first, see its potential right away, and then focus on how much they would like to get out of their garage. Other times, a leader recognizes an opportunity to disrupt a competitive marketplace, which usually requires a kind of exponentially quick scale-up that isn't possible without a rapid and ready influx of capital. In a service industry like mine, this kind of thing is rare, but if you're in technology or healthcare (among many other rapidly growing industries), professional money can be the surest way to reach the next level.

Bringing in a VC investor or group can be exactly what the doctor ordered in these circumstances. These relationships can be incredibly successful, provided you carefully vet and choose the right VC with the right skill set and sign a contract with appropriate financial terms and the proper distribution of control. VCs can bring huge amounts of talent and access to a network of customers that you might not have had otherwise. And one of the key strategic and operational benefits is speed to market of your product or service; however, all of these benefits come with a price. So you have to be sure that the value of the benefits is worth the potential future upside you are giving up. This is one of the trickiest and most emotional equations for a young entrepreneur. And it can be extremely tempting.

But a VC arrangement can also be dangerous if you don't know what you're getting into. Professional money comes with Big Brother in the room. Your capital isn't as tight, but you are now subject to other factors, like investment return and time horizon expectations. This can lead to new kinds of pressures. For instance, VCs are specifically in the business of making money on a company's growth, so often they will expect the business to double every couple of years during their holding period. If you're growing, then you have a happy, supportive, and fully committed partner. If you're not, then you suddenly have a partner who is more concerned about stopping the bleeding and protecting their investment than they are about steering your company back toward success. They almost always look for either a quick success or quick failure and won't stick around long with a flagging company.

Then there are the control factors. Without professional money, you're running the show. With professional money, you might feel like you're both an owner and an employee. You'll be much more subject to the whims of other decision makers—to the point where you have to play a little *Game of Thrones* with the board, the VCs, and the other shareholders. If you don't meet certain growth criteria, the investor might exercise their right to take control of the company. When this happens, you might find yourself demoted so a professional manager from the VC side can take over and attempt to right the ship.

My friend Ed Stack, Chairman and CEO of Dick's Sporting Goods, provides a great example of this potential danger in his book *It's How We Play The Game*.[10] His situation occurred in the early maturation phase of Dick's Sporting Goods, when he had taken on VC investors who encouraged rapid growth in store openings, which pushed the limit of the current lender's credit facility. Ed found himself in a catch-22. The new lender would not provide a facility large enough to meet the cash flow needs of the expansion without the VC investors putting in additional capital. Conversely, the VC investors wouldn't invest additional capital without the lender's commitment to a larger credit facility. The VC investors, realizing their leverage, negotiated additional equity and a controlling number of board seats. This is why we often say internally that venture capitalists can turn into vulture capitalists. How Ed eventually wrestled back board control and his entire entrepreneurial journey illustrates the extreme risk of taking professional money, touches on almost every emotion in the spectrum, and shows how long a stakeholder list can get.

Professional money will usually come with the least favorable terms for you as the entrepreneur because the person or group offering the capital will recognize how desperate you are for the money. They know

---

10 Ed Stack, *It's How We Play the Game: Build a Business. Take a Stand. Make a Difference.* (New York: Scribner, 2019).

that the statistics are against them for your success. VCs are quite aware of the fact that 75 percent of venture-backed businesses fail. For this reason, they're going to try to maximize the expected reward for the risk they're taking by investing in you. This means more equity for them than you might be comfortable with—especially after your company starts bringing in a huge return and you see how little of it you get to keep. Giving up equity early on can come with an extremely high cost.

When you take professional money, the most important thing is to go in with your eyes wide open and then make sure all the *I*s are dotted and *T*s crossed in the contract. As long as you know what you're up against in the event of flagging growth, and as long as you are willing to trade some of your equity and control of the company (either now or at a future date), then accepting VC funding can be the smoothest ride emotionally. There is certainly less fear and anxiety about the money itself, as you take yourself off the hook almost entirely. But your future earnings will suffer in exchange, and you will be far less flexible to pursue the avenues you want to pursue.

Emotional Lessons:

- Not everyone is a born entrepreneur or a natural leader. It takes humility to recognize your weaknesses and then develop, hire, or partner with someone who has the skill sets you need to take your business to the next level. Paul and Steve's bank recognized their complementary skills as being exactly what the flagging brokerage firm needed. Jeff Bezos saw an opportunity and pursued the correct avenue for the funding he needed to meet that opportunity. Young Steve Jobs failed to see the lessons he still needed to learn as a business manager and entrepreneur and wound up getting elbowed out by his company's board after it went public. He learned those lessons in the years that followed, which is what set him up so well for his triumphant return to Apple.

- It all starts with an honest self-assessment. Those who recognize their skill sets and limitations go on to create great things, but they almost always do so with the help of others. Don't fall victim to stubbornness, selfishness, hubris, or egotism. (I have met this kind of person, and they never lead their organization to its fullest potential.) Know your skills. Know your needs. Then seek the funding source best equipped to meet those specific needs.

Technical Strategies:

- Put together a great team of professionals to help provide your capital needs and protect your interest.
- Know where your funding is coming from and know what your capital costs you (both in current cash flow and potential future equity).
- Create the most detailed business plan you can, even if it's just you in your garage at the start. Keep in mind that whenever you bring in an outside investor, the growth trajectory expectations are completely different.
- As you move through capital and need additional funds, understand how those funds will be structured, and plan for those future needs.
- Be aware of exactly how much equity you're giving up in exchange for not having to worry about where you're going to get the capital your business needs.
- Be aware of exactly how much *control* you're giving up as well. This way, you can avoid the constant threat of somebody clawing back more of your equity and upside if you don't perform.

Strategize Your Capital

I cannot overemphasize the need to do a realistic capital needs analysis for your business venture. I have witnessed so many good business ideas and passionate new entrepreneurs being limited because the owner spent an inordinate amount of his or her time continuously raising capital. This distraction takes away from advancing the core entrepreneurial opportunity.

I know this is easier said than done, especially when the new entrepreneur does not have a financial background and is forced to learn as she goes. Again, my recommendation is to find qualified and experienced professionals to help you with your capital needs analysis and capital raise strategy. It will be time and money well spent.

Maturation

CHAPTER THREE

The Dark Ages of Growth

Stakeholders:

- ⊘ You
- ⊘ Your spouse
- ⊘ Your children
- ⊘ Your partners
- ⊘ Your investor(s) or banker(s)
- ⊘ The emergence of your employees

Emotions:

- ⊘ Fear of the unknown in this new phase you have entered
- ⊘ Anxiety triggered from all the new issues, decisions, and stakeholders to juggle
- ⊘ Insecurity that can (and sometimes needs to) turn into paranoia
- ⊘ Doubt in your ability to steer this larger ship through tighter straits in a rapidly changing current (you ask yourself, *Can I rise to these new challenges?*)

- Pressure introduced by the responsibility to new stakeholders (this is becoming about more than just you)
- Excitement generated from the traction you have created
- Trust is needed in your key people, or you will reach your capacity and your progress will be limited

Symptoms:

- Fear and doubt brought on by market pressures
- Increasing sense that you are overwhelmed by decisions
- A feeling that there is no guidebook for how to steer your business through this unpredictable period of growth
- Desire to satisfy your investors (get used to this one, because it will only get stronger and more complicated the more your business grows)
- Clear recognition of your self-awareness and trust in your inner voice
- An understanding that you must learn to compartmentalize

THINK ABOUT YOUR FAVORITE entrepreneurial success story. Who comes to mind? Whoever it happens to be, I bet I can guess a few things about the story. First, you probably have a pretty good idea of how this entrepreneur got his or her start. Some of the most celebrated successes involve the leader setting up shop in a garage. There's just something so appealing about the underdog who started on a shoestring budget with only a concept and a dream to guide the way. (Think about Russ hustling in the pool hall to make payroll.)

The other piece of the story that I can probably guess is that this entrepreneur became extremely wealthy as a result of the business. In some cases, the leader rose to the level of a global figure because he or she now runs one of the world's highest-profile companies. In others, the leader sold the business for $50 million, $100 million, $500 million, or more and is now retired and living the kind of life that allows him or her to pursue other passions.

We Can Learn from Those Who Have Failed

Typically, when we discuss these celebrated entrepreneurs and their companies, we tend to leave out the middle part of the story. We know quite a bit about the start and even more about the success at the end, but what about the many months, years, or even decades of growth between? The mythology almost never covers that part which is kind of crazy, because the middle part is often the longest, most challenging phase of the Entrepreneurial Lifecycle. Anyone hoping to emulate that celebrated entrepreneur would benefit *most* from learning about what this now-successful entrepreneur did during this highly difficult and typically unpredictable phase.

Further, these stories often suffer from survivorship bias. You hear plenty about the people who came out at the end as winners. But what about the ones who made it into the Maturation Phase, grew the business for a while, and then failed? Those stories are almost never studied. The truth is that we can learn just as much (if not more) from the leaders who had a great start-up before hitting the Maturation Phase and then languished.

Take it from Carl, whose story I mentioned previously, who experienced this very thing firsthand on two separate occasions when his companies filed for bankruptcy. I asked him what he learned from these experiences, and he shined plenty of light on what is often a dark time.

SUCCESS IN ONE ARENA DOES NOT NECESSARILY
TRANSFER TO ANOTHER

"Stick with what you know," he told me. For this client, it was the plastics and petrochemical industry. Trying to transition into winemaking, commercial real estate, and a consumer product business took him out of his element and put him into arenas that he didn't know enough about. When you find some success in one business, product or service line, or industry, it's easy to get wrapped up in the idea that you're a brilliant leader who can make any kind of business work, no matter what.

Even if you can control yourself enough to avoid jumping into new industries you know too little about, there is also the danger of assuming that your leadership is the sole reason the company is growing. If you get stuck in the mind-set of thinking that your decisions are always right, no matter what anyone else says, then eventually, one of those decisions will cost you. As my client told me, "For most entrepreneurs, finding humility can cost lots of money." Never forget that every successful business requires a little luck and plenty of help from others. Keep that humility close, because it could be the only thing that saves you from making rash decisions that lead to disaster.

NETWORKING IN ONE INDUSTRY DOES NOT
ALWAYS TRANSLATE TO ANOTHER

The second way that overconfidence can hinder a business venture is by assuming that your contacts in one industry or business will be able to help you grow in another industry or business. Even if you owe quite a bit of your success to your network (and even if some people in your network owe quite a bit of their success to you), their skills and connections aren't as likely to help you if or when you take on new ventures in different industries.

CAREFULLY VET YOUR PARTNERS

During the Maturation Phase, you face many decisions related to growth. In some cases, you reach a point where it becomes clear that you can't grow any further on your own, and you may have to take on a partner. As my client pointed out, before you bring on a partner, you have to make sure you know as much as you can about them. "I know of one great start-up that was ruined by an alcoholic partner who hid the disease well," my client explained. This company was on a seemingly unstoppable trajectory until "his lack of sobriety caused a terrible accident, almost killing an employee." The resulting legal fallout ruined the company.

"It took me two bankruptcies before I really accepted these lessons," my client admitted. "Fortunately, I did learn them, and the last chapter was a success!"

A huge part of why my client (and other entrepreneurs) have to learn these lessons the hard way is because there isn't much literature on the subject of the Maturation Phase. That's why the title of this chapter identifies this early portion of the Maturation Phase "the Dark Ages of Growth." Like the historical period of the same name, your business has now entered into an indeterminately long stretch about which little has been written. Of course, the goal is to become one of the celebrated few instead of the languishing many.

Take heart, because while the Maturation Phase might feel like those awkward middle school years, it is also where the wind really starts driving your sails. This is where great companies are made. This is where the stakes are highest for your business, for your stakeholders, and for yourself. Your decisions during this period will dictate the level of success your business achieves. Let's figure out where you and your business stand, so we can better ensure that those decisions are the *right* ones.

The Internal and External Threats

If the stories of entrepreneurs losing their momentum during the Maturation Phase teaches us anything, it's this: During this phase, you should never get too comfortable. Don't forget that the winds and currents are always unpredictable. Just because you have them figured out today doesn't mean they can't shift on you tomorrow. You have to keep your head on a swivel, because there are many *internal* and *external* threats that could completely change your trajectory. Change is the only constant.

INTERNAL THREATS

For the *internal* side of the equation, consider the story of Paul and Steve from the previous chapter, two partners who seized an incredible opportunity to inherit a flagging business that they ultimately wound up turning around. Paul and Steve came together quickly to capitalize on an opportunity to lead an international brokerage company that was about to default on its sixty-eight million pounds of debt before likely heading into bankruptcy. The two partners worked with the bank to restructure all the debt and become fifty-fifty owners. This left them to figure out how to turn it around, put in an operating agreement for governance, steer the business back toward solvency, and earn a healthy profit.

In the early days, it looked like an ideal partnership between two people with perfectly complementary skills. Paul was a workaholic and quite astute in executing of the company business, motivating the team, building culture, and generating profits. Paul has a lot of Emotional Intelligence (EI). He ran the New York division so efficiently that it quickly grew in both topline revenue and margin. Steve, meanwhile, was more skilled at corporate governance, so he ran the London division and began developing the operating governance.

In short order, the company started doing well enough to meet the aggressive principal paydown schedule set by the bank. It also generated cash flow in excess of debt coverage in order to provide for a nice executive compensation package, including travel on the Concorde, a corporate retreat home in Florida, and other attractive perks for both owners. The currents were heading in the right direction, and they had the wind at their backs. They were sailing smoothly through the middle of their Maturation Phase, and it looked like nothing could stop them.

Then tragedy struck: Paul had a heart attack. It was severe enough that he had to stay in the hospital for seven days and then spend several months in recovery.

During his recovery, two things happened: First, Paul's doctor advised him not to return to his high-stress Wall Street position, and second, pursuant to the terms of the operating agreement, the board, which was controlled by Steve, appointed Paul's interim replacement.

Paul was a high-energy and dynamic leader. Eight weeks later, when Paul felt like his old self again, he had the tough realization that at age forty-six he had to figure out what was next for him. He went through a period of depression.

So over the next six to twelve months, he and Steve explored different options, like developing a real estate division, an administrative management position, and other lower-stress roles. None of this satisfied Paul's Type A personality. He had to come to the realization that this traumatic health event would change his life and the future of the company forever.

Meanwhile, Paul retained his 50 percent ownership interest in the company. To Steve's credit, he continued to pay Paul his salary as his recovery continued. However, over the next twelve months, it became very clear that Steve wanted to buy out Paul's shares, and he made his dominant negotiating position clear.

Approximately eighteen months after Paul's heart attack, I was given the task of negotiating with Steve's representatives about the buyout of Paul's shares on his behalf. This proved to be a real challenge. I looked under every rock for any type of negotiating leverage. One thing we did have going for us was the backing of the lenders, who admired Paul's operating expertise and management charisma. With that, we were able to get a somewhat reasonable price and reach terms that Paul and Steve would execute to end the partnership. But in the process, Paul learned a hard lesson about the multitude of catastrophic threats any individual or company—even one that appears to be sailing smoothly—can face at any moment.

EXTERNAL THREATS

On the other end of the spectrum, our client Dan learned about a few often-overlooked *external* threats late in his Entrepreneurial Lifecycle. Here was a man who had fought and scraped to build his company into a juggernaut over the course of nearly six decades. He owed part of his success to a strategy he implemented during the Survival Phase, which was to pay down debt as aggressively as possible. Whenever he had the cash, he would always pay down debt in advance.

Then, right when his company was getting some major traction, a recession hit. His cash flow plummeted, and because of his aggressive debt repayment tendencies, he had no cash reserves. *It's okay*, he thought. *We'll weather this storm. I am way ahead on my bank payments, so I can miss a few.* Well, the bank doesn't view things that way. Since he didn't have the cash reserved to make current payments, he nearly had his entire business taken away. To avoid the disaster, he had to scramble to get another lender on board to take out the current bank. He learned a valuable cash management lesson the hard way.

The external economic factors taught him a key lesson: When you reach Maturation, you can't keep running your business like it's a start-up. You need to learn different cash management skills. Dan now watches debt coverage ratios and cash reserves, and most importantly, he learned to read external signal indicators that can predict when an economic downturn is on the horizon. That experience made his economic radar as keen as anyone's I have seen.

These lessons teach us two things: First, there are both *internal* and *external* threats to any business, no matter how much traction it has or growth it's enjoying; second (and most importantly), you never know when these threats will hit you or where they will come from. In the Entrepreneurial Lifecycle, the phases don't always happen in linear order, and the threats are unpredictable. To avoid them, it helps to learn from those who have come before you.

The Velocity of Decision-Making

Over the years, I have witnessed a great variety of decision-making processes used by individuals from different industries, with different educational backgrounds, approaching decisions of different magnitudes. Here, we revisit Dan, who has always had a lot of angst about his education level. He often says, "I always wonder what I could have accomplished if . . ." The reality is that he has the highest EI of anyone I know—especially in terms of his self-awareness, self-motivation, relationship handling, and recognizing and managing the emotions of others. This all made him an inspiring leader with a clear vision and a passion to achieve it. Therefore, others would trust and follow him.

It is my belief that people like him, those with high EI, develop a key trait that allows them to make better decisions. I call this trait the *Velocity of Decision-Making*. The term implies the *process* and not merely the *speed* at which we make decisions. A high Velocity of Decision-Making allows great leaders to rely on more than simply their IQ, even as they manage multiple inputs from themselves and others, control their impulse tendencies, and maintain a keen self-awareness that gives them confidence to decide and act.

Former Secretary of State Colin Powell once suggested that if you're going to make a proper decision, you need somewhere between 40 percent and 70 percent of the information available.[11] If you decide

---

11 General Colin Powell, "A Leadership Primer," accessed June 23, 2019, https://www.slideshare.net/guesta3e206.

before you reach 40 percent, you've decided too early, and if you wait around to get *all* the information you think you need, it's too late—the opportunity will have passed you by. This is profound wisdom, and it absolutely implies that your inner voice, your experiential wisdom, and even your *gut* must be present in all your decision-making. We'll discuss this concept more in the next chapter, but for now, keep in mind that the gut feelings, which often guide your decisions in the end, should never be ignored.

The most successful entrepreneurs have a high level of confidence in their gut and experiential wisdom. This allows them to weigh the exact balance of the empirical data required, coupled with their instincts, in order to definitively make decisions. Past decisions, right or wrong, build up that experiential wisdom. "You learn more from mistakes than from successes!" This statement is absolutely true. Conversely, if you dwell in the past and lament the wrong decisions you've made, it can negatively affect your confidence in your instincts, which therefore slows your Velocity of Decision-Making. My own experiential gut wisdom tells me that billions of dollars are lost or gained annually based not on right or wrong choices but on the velocity of those decisions.

So how do we get to where we're balancing properly between experiential wisdom and empirical information? How do we achieve that perfect symmetry between EI and IQ and find the perfect *velocity*? In the chapters to come, we will explore these questions and build on the critical characteristics of Velocity of Decision-Making, a trait that stays with successful leaders through all phases of the entrepreneurial journey. We'll discuss how a huge component is paying close attention to both the *internal* and *external* forces that could disrupt your traction and slow your growth. But the process starts with learning from those who have come before you. Accepting their wisdom as part of your own is the purest antidote to these Dark Ages of growth.

Intriguing Insights from Successful Entrepreneurs

When we interviewed our entrepreneurial clients about their journeys through the business lifecycle, a few common themes emerged. One of them is that many of our clients wish they'd had a certain skill set earlier in the Maturation Phase. They enjoyed considerable growth and met with a great deal of success during this phase, but if they had been better in that one key area, they might have avoided mistakes or enjoyed an even better rate of growth.

For one client, it was mentorship. For another, it was the speed and process for hiring and firing. (Incidentally, this was the toughest lesson for me to learn as well.) Still another discussed how he'd picked his attorney based solely on a personal relationship rather than professional expertise and wound up wishing he'd had better legal advice (which speaks to one of my favorite sayings: "There is nothing more expensive than bad legal advice!" *So true*).

In search of these common themes, we asked a simple but insightful question of clients who have built successful and high-profile businesses across a range of industries: If you could go back in time, what advice would you give to your younger self? While the individual answers varied, four major themes emerged.

RELATIONSHIPS ARE MORE IMPORTANT THAN YOUR PRODUCT OR SERVICE

Nearly every business owner and entrepreneur we interviewed mentioned a desire to have spent more time on relationships. Most often, they wished they had focused more on their relationships with their employees—especially during the early portion of the Maturation Phase, when you're working with employees who will eventually become management as your company grows.

With the benefit of hindsight, many recognized the incredible value of having a positive and cohesive team. Others wondered what might have been had they concentrated more energy and attention on identifying the attributes of ideal candidates who would perform the quality of work desired while also seamlessly fitting into the company's culture. Later, after selling or transitioning their business, many wished that they could have offered greater reward in the form of equity to the people who had contributed so much to the company's growth.

Sometimes, you get so focused on what you think you *should* be doing that you miss opportunities to develop or hire for skills that could help your business or organization in overlooked areas. For example, maybe you're being influenced from a purely financial perspective and keeping payroll at a certain level when you should instead be concentrating on objective evaluation of the cultural fit of each employee and their potential contribution to the team. Focusing too much on the bottom line or even being influenced by your emotional connection to a particular employee or employees can often cloud your judgment and blind you to the best courses of action.

My philosophy is that people are *everything*. Even if it feels like you can't afford more employees, you have to be opportunistic. When good talent is available, and they are a good cultural fit, you must hire them even if it will blow that year's budget and you aren't at a point of capacity where you can utilize their talent 100 percent. The mind-set has to be this: We are a committed, growing company, and we will grow into the need. Conversely, if you wait until you are at capacity, then the field of potential candidates is more limited, and you must act quickly to relieve the stress created by thin capacity. Public companies can't take that short-term hit to earnings, but private entrepreneurial companies have the luxury of long-term vision.

Relationships outside the business were deemed to be just as important. Many of our clients wished that they had spent more time developing their professional networks and aligning with strategic partners. Better relationships with internal partners was frequently mentioned as something these entrepreneurs were missing too. Strong relationships with stakeholders can also greatly benefit a growing company, both at work and at home. These relationships, after all, are what you lean on when you're facing a difficult decision. The closer you are to these key people, the more collective the insight becomes, the better your Velocity of Decision-Making, and the more likely you are to make the *right* decision.

Further, as a company evolves and its market changes, its reliance on a product or service to drive the success of the company also changes. Competition has a tendency to disrupt product or service differentiation. When this happens, those key relationships become especially important to help the company's leaders evolve alongside the market. This is one of those aspects of running a business where Emotional Intelligence is particularly important.

YOUR COMFORT ZONE IS YOUR ENEMY

The majority of business owners and entrepreneurs that we've worked with share the notion that their businesses wound up looking quite a bit different than their original vision. You never know what obstacles you will face or what opportunities will arise. Then there are always the winds of emotion and the currents of market factors pulling you in directions you didn't anticipate. All these driving influences tend to lead businesses down unintended paths. Often, the ones that fail are those led by an entrepreneur who refuses to adapt to new headwinds and instead tries to steer the ship back into the waves (i.e., he or she hasn't yet developed their sense of *external* vision nor confidence in that *gut* feeling). A slow Velocity of Decision-Making can also sink ships.

Even in the cases where a business succeeds, its leader often expresses regret for not seeing the need to take a new direction earlier. Nearly all the entrepreneurs we interviewed said that they wished they had pushed themselves out of their comfort zones earlier in the Maturation Phase, because it would have accelerated their growth.

What does getting outside your comfort zone look like? Usually it involves taking on more risk. In the Survival Phase, it often feels like you're *living* on risk, so once you move into Maturation, the tendency is to take a break from risk for a while (sometimes for too long). It's only natural to get a little worn down by the chances you've had to take. But make no mistake, the Maturation Phase is not the time to quit taking risks. Just because you're enjoying a healthy cash flow, that doesn't mean you've reached your destination. Growth requires risk. Remember, if you're not growing, you're dying.

Risk aversion is a natural survival instinct, but it won't help your company endure. In nearly every case, our entrepreneur clients said they wished they had been more willing (particularly early in the Maturation Phase) to push themselves outside their comfort zones and take chances. This is because, over the years, they learned that great success does not come without bold action. You just have to trust yourself and your intuition, try new strategies, and never be afraid to make bold decisions.

To compel a healthier level of risk-taking in my own company, I created a research and development line item that the new leadership team *must* spend on new technology, new strategies, new *whatever*. They're not penalized for using these funds for ideas that don't pan out; they're only penalized if they don't spend it. I fully expect that 65 percent or more of that budget will go to unsuccessful experiments, but the cost is worth it, because it forces everyone to think outside their comfort zone and to come up with creative ideas. I want to have a culture where failure is okay, even celebrated. If you aren't making mistakes, you aren't trying hard enough.

EMBRACE YOUR ADD

I believe that I have some level of ADD. I had always considered it a handicap until one day at a coaching session a colleague made a sarcastic remark about his own ADD. Everyone laughed until the coach brought a serious tone to the room by explaining his experience with his entrepreneurial clients, who numbered in the thousands. "Who here has been diagnosed with or believe they have ADD to some degree?" he asked the people in the room. Approximately two-thirds of the attendees raised a hand.

"I ask this question at all my sessions," he explained, "and the percentages are consistent."

We spent the next hour discussing why this might be and why having ADD might help the entrepreneurial journey. In my view, entrepreneurs who embrace their ADD are able to switch more naturally between managing the multitude of *internal* and *external* threats. This makes them better equipped to recognize that some things are outside their control, which allows them to focus on only those matters they *can* control. They have developed a higher level of comfort in their EI, reliance on their gut and experiential wisdom, and thus a higher Velocity of Decision-Making. All of this puts them in a strong position to successfully navigate the currents of the Maturation Phase.

DON'T LOOK BACK

A key concept you can use to keep your Velocity of Decision-Making where it needs to be is to never look back. Once you've made your decision, stick to it. The road to success is littered with second-guessing. When you're making decisions based on intuition, there's always going to be some questioning about whether you made the right choice. Could something have been done earlier? Better? More effectively? Of course, but just like its leader(s), no business is perfect.

If you allow these questions to spur regrets, you risk blurring your vision for the future and slowing your Velocity of Decision-Making. The more time you spend looking back, the less time you have to look forward. That was an overriding theme we found when we spoke to our interviewees: No one held any long-term regrets. They choose to think about the positive in what they learned, as opposed to regretting miscalculations. Some suggested that they could have made different choices or done something earlier, but everyone took comfort in the knowledge that their insight and persistence carried the business to the ultimate goal. As one longtime executive asserted, "Brilliant people are wrong 50 percent of the time."

If you are likely to be wrong 50 percent of the time, there must be some measure of luck that comes into play. Being at the right place at the right time is very much a part of the Entrepreneurial Lifecycle. But more important is the entrepreneur's skill set, dedication, persistence, boldness, and *internal* and *external* vision. If you form the right relationships and nurture them, opportunities will arise. Then it is up to you to be bold enough to seize those opportunities, never rest in contentment, and then never look back.

Emotional Lessons:

- Embrace your ADD. Managing multiple challenges and opportunities simultaneously is a strength, not a weakness.
- Don't take your foot off the gas—as your business starts to mature, the same winds and currents as before can knock you off course.

Technical Strategies:

- Watch out for false signals. During the Maturation Phase, there are many signals that come at you from all directions. You must develop your own radar system to determine which signals are real and which signals are not.
- Develop your Velocity of Decision-Making.

- Don't be afraid of making mistakes; learn from them.
- Don't let a fear of mortality or hubris delay proper contingency planning. Take the time to plan for health problems, tragedy, or other potential threats that could interrupt your entrepreneurial journey. Too often this type of planning is ignored entirely with the reasoning "It will never happen to me." But in Paul's situation, it most certainly did, and it changed the course of his life.

Stay the Course

As you pull yourself out of the Dark Ages and progress through the Maturation Phase, your business will begin to get some serious traction. For a while, it will feel like you've made it—like all your problems are behind you. But as I mentioned earlier, there is no such thing as smooth sailing. Keeping your ship on the right course will require a keen *internal* focus (the ability to read your own emotions and heighten your Velocity of Decision-Making) and *external* vision (the ability to see changing winds and currents in the industry in which you operate).

With better understanding of these internal and external factors, you will develop an almost clairvoyant ability to identify risks and opportunities that lie ahead, and in a *timely* fashion. Knowing these risks and opportunities well in advance makes you a better leader, one who can manage a team to execute your strategies, capture opportunities, and diminish risks. This is the surest route from beginning Maturation to a lucrative Transition.

CHAPTER FOUR

Gaining Traction

Stakeholders:

- ✓ You
- ✓ Your spouse
- ✓ Your children
- ✓ Your partners
- ✓ Your investor(s) or banker(s)
- ✓ Your employees
- ✓ Clients or customers
- ✓ Advisors and consultants
- ✓ Attorneys
- ✓ Your partner's partners
- ✓ Key management employees

Emotions:

- ✓ Confidence and doubt
- ✓ Trust and distrust
- ✓ Security and greed
- ✓ Anticipation and hubris
- ✓ Arrogance and insecurity
- ✓ Loneliness and comfort in the team

Symptoms:

- ✓ Talking to yourself frequently
- ✓ Questioning your vision (and sometimes your sanity)
- ✓ A longing to spend more time in your comfort zone
- ✓ Difficulty with taking time away from work
- ✓ People may start to label you as a control freak
- ✓ Stress related to the prospect of giving up some control and responsibility

IMAGINE THAT YOU'RE MERGING onto a busy highway. The traffic is thick and roaring past at Autobahn speeds. Everyone seems more concerned about the phone call they're on or the text they're reading than avoiding a fiery death under a jackknifing eighteen-wheeler. We've all been there. Merging into this kind of traffic can require a leap of faith. It's certainly difficult, as you have to keep yourself on high alert, check every angle for signs of danger and risk, and then time things perfectly.

Starting a business is similar. At first, merging into an existing market is tough. You feel like a catastrophic collision could happen at any moment and could come from any direction. With all these risks swirling around, your strategy is usually to simply rocket forward as fast as you can. It seems so terrifying and so difficult, but weirdly, once you're in the market, you realize that the real challenge is still ahead of you. Now you have to navigate traffic. You can't simply floor it. You must regulate your pace and bob and weave around the other competitors, regulatory changes, and challenges that fly into your lane.

So the big question is this: How the hell do you do all that and still keep your mind (and for that matter, your sanity) in check? Self-awareness, self-control, and the appropriate Velocity of Decision-Making. Yes, you need drive, motivation, skill, and money to succeed. But equally important is your ability to control yourself and your emotions once your business starts to get traction. So, let's turn our attention to the *internal* factors. Let's examine how to manage yourself and your time and focus your attention so you can position your business for controlled, sustainable growth through the Maturation Phase.

Listen to Yourself

You know that voice in your head that you converse with sometimes? Don't worry; we all do it. Some people call it a conscience. Others call it intuition. The new and trendy term is "mindfulness." Some refer to it as "your gut." I call it your "inner voice." For those who are solo start-up entrepreneurs, their inner voice becomes their most trusted confidante. Your inner voice helps you personally deal with rapidly changing circumstances and balance your ethical, emotional, and logical responses.

During the Maturation Phase, that inner voice has a way of becoming your best friend. It keeps you inside the guardrails, helps contain your emotional reactions so they don't override your logic, and most importantly, ensures that your moral compass always remains pointed true north. Another benefit is this: You probably don't know a lot of people you can have conversations with about your ideas and doubts regarding your business, so your inner voice serves as a valuable sounding board. You might have a partner—and if so, that's great. You're fortunate to be able to conduct some of these conversations with another human once in a while. But if you're starting this business on your own, it's just you and your inner voice.

Unfortunately, the inner voice can sometimes fail to keep you on the correct path. My premise is that our complex emotional hardwiring has every bit as much (if not more) to do with our success or failure as our logical business decision-making. If we allow our amygdala to override our frontal lobe, our emotions hit an extreme, and then things can quickly go wrong. This is what Dr. Goleman calls an "amygdala hijack."

I have seen fear and anxiety make good people with great ideas give up on their businesses. I have seen people who couldn't trust others and therefore significantly limited their potential. I have seen hubris neuter the logical thought process and lead many to overextend themselves or wander in inadvisable directions without the disciplined caution that got them to where they were in the first place. When this happens, without that inner voice to restore balance in a timely fashion, it can kill the business.

As I mentioned previously, one of the best things you can do as an entrepreneur is spend time outside your comfort zone. Taking risks is the surest way to grow. But it sure can be lonely out there. It's just you— you and your inner voice.

Your inner voice can challenge you. It can be the one thing that reminds you about the merits of what you're doing, that without risk there can be no reward, and that you have the skills and knowledge necessary to grow this business into something far bigger than yourself. It can also be that voice of reason to keep hubris, greed, distrust, and other negative impulses in check.

It's easy enough to know which kind of inner voice you're dealing with when it actually uses *words* inside your head. But sometimes, the inner voice is just a feeling in your gut. For instance, if today felt *really good* even though you didn't actually accomplish anything on your to-do list, then it's probably because your inner voice is silently telling you that it's so warm and cozy in your comfort zone. The general sense is that you can't fail if you don't try.

This voice can drive you, or it can drive you crazy. If you're going to be on good terms with your inner voice, then you need to feel a little uncomfortable (and sometimes, you need to feel *a lot* uncomfortable). The voice should be a good coach, a tough coach, and a motivating coach. It must be willing to call you out during those times when you start to get too comfortable. Every day should bring new challenges. Occasionally those challenges will overwhelm you. Sometimes you'll succeed and sometimes you'll fail, but what matters most is that your inner voice keeps you *accountable* to the goals you're trying to accomplish.

Achieve Self-Awareness (Get to Know Yourself)

Listening to your inner voice is only the first step. The next step is recognizing that the inner voice (and your reliance upon it) will change, along with everything else, as you move through the Maturation Phase. In the coming months and years, the more your business grows, the more employees and stakeholders you will take on. This will complicate the emotional and technical matrix. Having strong self-awareness will give you confidence and conviction in your plan to get there, even as you introduce the opinions, behaviors, talents, and emotional complexities of others. Traffic is getting fast and thick now, but you have a feel for the wheel.

Here's the thing to keep in mind, though: Unlike your inner voice, those real, live people you surround yourself with tend to talk back. Sometimes their advice is good. Other times, not so much. This is another reason to keep from silencing your inner voice. It's that essential check and balance, that component of yourself that helps you filter the good advice from the bad—the positive influences from the negative, the great ideas from the shortsighted ones—all while keeping your emotional triggers under control.

It's like the great athletes who say that no one—not even the world's best coach—can motivate them as well as they can motivate themselves. This is because a coach will shake his or her head, yell at you, and then move on to the other players and the next play. But your inner voice is a lot less forgiving. An honest inner voice, along with the *keen self-awareness* to listen to it, will always tell you what went wrong, and if you listen hard enough (meaning don't make excuses to silence it), it will also show you how to avoid making that mistake again and how to get back up and try a new strategy next time. Your inner voice will hold you accountable if you let it.

Your Most Impactful Stakeholder

While we're on the subject of self-discovery and (consciously or subconsciously) learning how to deal with emotions in conditions that you've never experienced before in life, let's talk about loneliness. Before this point in the Lifecycle, it's likely that anxiety, fear, and insecurity left no room for loneliness. Now, though, there's a good chance you're feeling the weight of it. Several of our entrepreneur clients have ranked this condition at the top of their list of difficulties. This is because when you're the leader of a business—particularly during the Maturation Phase—you alone are responsible for your actions and decisions (especially when they start to impact employees, loved ones, and other stakeholders).

This is why I can't stress enough the importance of your most impactful stakeholder: your spouse, significant other, or partner. If you have a partner who is in sync with you and 100 percent supportive, it is the most valuable asset you could wish for. I've known individuals who did and those who did not have that solid relationship and supportive partner. The worst-case scenario involves a divorce, an occurrence that can be an emotional cyclone in itself—one that often runs parallel with the other emotional challenges of running a business. When divorce happens, the business may struggle or not survive.

On the positive side, when we see situations where business leaders have a supportive and pragmatic partner, negative emotions are extinguished by positive reinforcement. This enhances the entrepreneur's energy, focus, creativity, and leadership charisma. I am one of those fortunate ones. My wife, Maureen, has been nothing but supportive. She has been that rock for me in those difficult times, the one who makes them short and shallow. Whenever I look back on the darkest, toughest times, I always recall talking through things with Maureen and getting nothing but unconditional support and confidence back from her. I have three sons who work in the business, and all three of them will tell you that, like a broken record, an insight I frequently share is that "one of the most important decisions you'll ever make in life is who you marry." The right partner significantly minimizes the effects of loneliness on your leadership journey.

I once asked a good friend and successful entrepreneur this question: "What was the toughest thing about being a sole-owner entrepreneur?" "The toughest thing was that I didn't have much choice," he told me. "I was in the infancy of the new and fast-growing business, so I had no one to bounce ideas off of. I felt alone. I didn't have a mentor. I felt isolated and uncertain about all the decisions I had to make." The value of having a trusted partner as a spouse cannot be calculated.

Finding Your Own Management Style

Once you have confidence in yourself and clarity in your vision, your business will gain the kind of traction that will require you to bring in more and more employees. During this period, the number one rule of success is this: Your people are everything.

This can be an easy lesson to forget when the lines are still blurred between Survival and Maturation. Even at this point, if you're not fully in tune with your inner voice and the *internal* threats your business faces, the tendency is to continue fighting your fight to refine your product or service, manage cash flow, and try to wear all the hats even while your team is expanding. Many entrepreneurs hold on too long to their control over the purchasing, human resources, or production departments, among others, while their team expands.

While all of this is going on, another important thing is happening without you even knowing it: You've entered the early stages of developing your management and leadership style. First, let me make one key distinction: Management and leadership are two very different and equally important things. According to the *Harvard Business Review*, "Management consists of controlling a group or a set of entities to accomplish a goal. Leadership refers to an individual's ability to influence, motivate, and enable others to contribute toward organizational success. Influence and inspiration separate leaders from managers, not power and control."[12]

While managers plan, organize, coordinate, and measure tasks to accomplish projects, leaders inspire, mentor, and motivate their followers to create a vision for the organization. The former requires skills like strategic thinking, problem-solving, and organization. The latter requires motivation, delegation, encouragement, and creativity.

Whether you realized it or not, your development of all these skills began in the Survival Phase. Now, as you move through Maturation, your company's success or failure will depend on how you allow these skills to blossom. Leaning too heavily on management skills can blur your company's broader vision and stall its growth. Leaning too heavily on leadership skills can make your company inspired but directionless. Put simply, you can't have one without the other and expect to maintain traction.

Fortunately, the two roles and all their accompanying skills are intertwined. Leadership starts with management. Meanwhile, management starts with knowing yourself.

Be Transparent

Make transparency and candor part of your company culture. Numerous times throughout the day, I am reminded of the book *Radical*

---

12 Vineet Nayar, "Three Differences Between Managers and Leaders," *Harvard Business Review*, August 2, 2013, https://hbr.org/2013/08/tests-of-a-leadership-transiti.

Candor: Be a Kick-Ass Boss without Losing Your Humility by Kim Scott.[13] Whether you're working with a partner, an employee, a customer, or a vendor, successful leaders seek that same high level of communication and transparency. This is the bedrock of leadership, emotional intelligence, and sustainable growth. People slip into patterns early, so the sooner you establish open, honest communication in your work and personal relationships (particularly with your spouse and kids), the stronger your relationships will be.

It's also highly beneficial to get familiar with your stakeholders' emotional composition. The more transparent you are, the more transparency you will receive in return. This allows you to get to know the goals that are driving your stakeholders' behaviors and expectations and to interact more harmoniously. This is particularly valuable information to have in partnership situations, and it becomes critically important during the Transition Phase. People change, and so do their priorities and tolerances. Without knowing where your stakeholders stand emotionally, you might find yourself surprised about how drastically those priorities and emotions have evolved when you go from Survival to Maturation.

Some clients of ours who own larger businesses have also found it useful to set up an advisory board. Traditionally, such a board is designed to provide strategic advice to a company's leadership on an informal level. This makes it a perfect setting to allow your key stakeholders (and anyone else in your circle whose opinions you trust) to share their thoughts and feelings about matters the company is currently facing. Not only does this allow everyone to have their voices heard, but it also broadens your insight into how to lead your company.

---

13 Kim Scott, *Radical Candor: Be a Kick-Ass Boss without Losing Your Humility* (New York: St. Martin's Press, 2017).

Set the Right Volume Control

It might seem counterintuitive, but a huge part of knowing yourself is recognizing the needs of the people around you. As you start to get traction and experience growth, it's so easy to lose yourself in the day-to-day demands of your business. Often, a driven entrepreneur will chalk up the time lost with loved ones as simply part of the sacrifice one has to make to grow a healthy business.

On top of that, technology makes it even more difficult to ever truly check out of work. Jim Scalo, CEO of Burns Scalo Real Estate in Pittsburgh, Pennsylvania, shared a great line about the impact of technology on modern life with me: "Twenty years ago, work was like a switch. You turned it on when you arrived at work, and then, at the end of the day, you turned it off and went home. But now, with the constant connectivity that technology provides, there's no such thing as turning work completely on or completely off. The blend of work and life is so constant and complete that it has become more like a volume switch. You're always connected to work, even in your personal life; and you're always connected to your personal life, even when you're at work. Wherever you happen to be at the time, you have to decide where to set that volume between your focus on work and your focus on life."

Most entrepreneurs I know spend their whole careers and most of their free time with their work volume knob set on a high, which lessens the sounds they pick up on in other areas of their life. That might seem like the right play. Building a business is difficult and time-consuming. It's easy to convince yourself that the noise from work is more important than family dinner conversations or being on time for the kids' baseball games. Advice: Set the work volume very low when you are with your family.

I have asked many of our most successful clients this question: "Looking back, what is the one thing you would have done differently?" Each of them said, "I would have spent more time at home with my family." Probably the most valuable lesson I learned early on was that I had to listen to my inner voice when it held me accountable to balance the volume between what I heard at work and what I heard at home.

The toughest part about the Maturation Phase is that if you haven't already started to sacrifice your personal time and energy, you will once your business gets some traction. Pivoting from survival to growth is incredibly challenging, and with that challenge comes greater sacrifice. It's easy to let the business consume you because you're trying to manage resources as efficiently as possible. You don't have enough employees. Cash is starting to flow, but there are suddenly more demands on that cash. All that time you used to have to dedicate to keeping the business afloat now shifts to even more time-intensive demands. Suddenly you're running development, finance, administration, billing and collections, strategic planning, market research, technology, sales and marketing, and human resources. An interesting trend that I am seeing is that today's Generation X and Y entrepreneurs seem to be more aware of the effect that this can have on personal relationships, but no matter what generation you're from, there is still only so much time in a day.

Don't Cheat on Your Spouse with the Business

All those long days and late nights you spend at work can make your spouse start to feel like they're sharing you with another great love. Similarly, if you have children, it's not uncommon for them to grow up thinking of "the business" as your favorite child. If you don't find ways to make time—quality, focused time where you're not thinking about work—with the people you love, then those relationships will suffer. I've seen entrepreneurs lose marriages over their dedication to their businesses, and I have seen children estranged from their parents for the same reason.

Yes, it's important to work hard and maintain your entrepreneurial drive, but you also have to remind yourself of the subtle but incredibly important difference between passion and love. Your business is a passion; your family is love. Always remember what you love most and who it is you're building this business for. Your family should always take priority.

Sometimes this might sound impossible. At the end of most days, it's difficult to scrape together the energy to spend quality time with your spouse and children. But if you hope to keep your business and your family in harmony throughout the Lifecycle of your business, it has to be done. You must find ways to dedicate time to the people you love in addition to the business about which you are so passionate. Rely on your inner voice to keep yourself accountable to your family.

I have clients who have dedicated vacation time to spend with their family every year as a rule. Another makes a point of not working on his children's birthdays so his children recognize that they will always be more important to him than his day-to-day business responsibilities. Still others will partner with their spouses on the business so they have a deeper understanding of the stresses and triumphs both at work and at home. This kind of partnership can be dangerous, as money and emotion are so inextricably linked, but when it works, it can be incredibly positive.

There are plenty of other ways to share your business-related experiences with your spouse without having to bring him or her into the leadership structure. All those ways involve making time and being open and honest. If you can be honest and vulnerable with your partner about your fears and struggles, they can be a valuable sounding board for you.

The Dangers of Business Addiction

Picture a drug addict. What do you imagine drives this person every day? The story of most drug addicts is that they get so intensely dependent that they sacrifice their finances, sleep, health, and personal relation-ships so they can single-mindedly pursue the comfort of the drug. Does any of that sound familiar? In the Survival Phase, you often have to sac-rifice your personal finances and sleep, and if you're not careful, you also sacrifice healthy eating habits, exercise, and your personal relationships, too. This might sound like an overly harsh comparison, but it is war-ranted. I have seen firsthand the destruction that business addictions can cause to individuals, families, and children.

Becoming addicted to the business is so easy. To avoid falling into this trap, think about your entrepreneurial life as a three-legged stool. Your business is only one leg of the stool. Your family represents another. And the final leg is your health. To achieve balance and harmony in your life, you have to make sure that all three legs get an equal portion of your attention. Remember the story of Paul, who had a heart attack at age forty-six. This was also after a divorce.

If you commit to balancing the attention you devote to your busi-ness, your family, and your health, the effort forces you to *trust* in other emerging leaders and *delegate* to them. Trust and delegation are abso-lutely critical conditions that have to exist in order for the organization to continue to grow. (For more on the subjects of trust and delegation, please see chapter 5.)

Nature, Nurture, and Control

Part of what drives people to become entrepreneurs is that they prefer to be in control. There's something so compelling about never hav-ing to answer to a boss. The problem with preferring control is that you can easily go too far and become a control *freak*. The difference between wanting things done your way and *requiring* them to be done your way is difficult to spot at first—particularly when you're the one doing the requiring.

The question is this: Is being a control freak nature or nurture? Are you born that way, or do you become that way? During the Maturation Phase, entrepreneurs will revert to control freak tendencies in part because they feel like it's their ass on the line and that no one else has to suffer the downside of the risks they face. From what I've observed, organizations can have many control freaks because there can be many people who feel like they have everything to lose. But if you look at any business, the person most often *labeled* the control freak is the one who feels like he or she has the most to lose.

If you've been described as a control freak, take heart in the idea that you're not alone. Don't forget about your inner voice and the voice of your most impactful stakeholder. On occasion, Maureen will look at me with one eyebrow raised and say, "John, you're being a control freak." Even when it's true, I would prefer to receive this information from my inner voice than from my wife's outer voice, but that's not always how it happens.

But how do you give up being a control freak? After all, aren't entrepreneurs and business leaders at least slightly controlling by nature? It starts by recognizing that you can't control everything. The effort extends to accepting outside help. In my case, I looked to two sources, to Dan Sullivan, founder of Strategic Coach, and to a few industry colleagues who were going through the same experience. Thanks to their combined insight into leveraging the unique skills of your management team (which I discuss in the next chapter), I ended up delegating and developing in two phases.

In the first phase, I delegated the responsibility of executing our various departments' services to our clientele. Before, I had managed most of the day-to-day responsibility for client relationships and the implementation of our services. Now these tasks could be managed and executed by key management team members. The second phase involved delegating the effort of strategic planning. For the next five to seven years, I worked with the management team so they could take on more responsibilities related to the strategic vision and strategic plan creation for the company.

In the next chapter, you'll learn how and when we executed these phases, but for now, it is time to begin accepting that every great business reaches this point. Whether you are successful in your efforts to delegate will depend on the abilities of your leadership team and the effectiveness of your methodology—and just as importantly, how readily you embrace that methodology.

I won't sugarcoat it: This isn't easy. Giving up control is one of the most difficult things an entrepreneur ever has to do. Perhaps you believe that you—and only you—knows what works best for this business. Only you have experienced this from the beginning. Only you have been through all this before. Only you can know the best answer every time. How could you ever be 100 percent sure that someone else can live up to that standard?

You can see the flaw in this logic right away. No one is right all the time. If you don't believe me, try telling your spouse that you're always right and see what happens. No one can ever be 100 percent sure of their decisions all the time. And even you have made mistakes along the way—that is part of what makes your business as strong as it is. Yes, this step will be difficult. But letting go of some of this control, delegating responsibilities to trusted stakeholders, and embracing the possibility of failure once in a while is a huge part of what will improve traction and drive growth during the Maturation Phase.

Emotional Lessons:

- Be open and honest with your spouse or partner about your fears and challenges so they can help you navigate tough challenges.

- Let your inner voice hold you accountable.

- Set your business's volume control on low when you are with the family. Learn from the millennial generation about balance.

- You've invested so much of yourself into your business; invest in your personal relationships as well. Of course, the most important personal relationship is with your spouse. When it comes to your spouse, it's easy to become so focused on your respective careers and home lives that you eventually don't even know each other. Sometimes you don't see it happening until the kids move out of the house and you're faced with the stark reality that the two of you have nothing to talk about. Allocate time to your spouse and children. Talk to each other. Eat together. Play together. Plan vacations together. Spend quality time.

- Talk to your children about your business. Even after working with hundreds of successful entrepreneurs, it never ceases to amaze me how someone can spend their whole lives building something that will ensure their children's financial future and then not spend a single moment talking to those children about *why* their mother or father spends so much time at work, *why* the business is important, and *how* to manage the money it affords the family. A business is like anything else in life; if you don't talk to your children about what it means, then your children will arrive at their own (often incorrect) conclusions. The more you discuss your work life with your kids, the more they will understand the sacrifices you make—and more importantly, *why* you make them. At Waldron Private Wealth, we have an entire service offering dedicated to helping clients with this issue. And it is one of the most common requests for help that our clients make.

Technical Strategies:

- Know the influences that your stakeholders' stakeholders may have on the business. If you have a partner, for example, that partner's spouse can become a dominant stakeholder over time. I have seen spouses gain so much control over the decision-making process that one partner feels like the other partner is just a proxy for his or her spouse. One client calls his partner's spouse a ventriloquist!

- You have a business plan; create a family plan. Having a family plan ensures that your personal goals are being met alongside your business goals. Effective family plans always include a predetermined goal for time off, time exclusively for your spouse, time for the children, and just as importantly, time for yourself (that doesn't involve the business). It often helps to establish boundaries on technology use and time spent traveling on business. Create a rigid and reinforced structure, a predefined set of rules. And make sure that everyone at your business knows how much you value your family plan—it is equally as important as your business plan.

- You have a vision for your business; you should have one for your family, too. We start every client relationship by asking, "What is your family vision?" Many clients quickly realize that they have never given this question a moment's thought. But the ones with strong relationships are always able to identify their vision and to make it central to their planning. The family vision should be similar to a mission statement: a short but meaningful definition of what your family is all about.

Embrace Trust, and Delegate

If your business is like a car on the highway, then the safest play is to always know the speed limit. To this point, the only thing you've been doing is accelerating, but speed alone doesn't win races. You have to navigate the turns with agility. And there are many turns as we move through the Maturation Phase. In the years to come, steady, sustainable growth is what will keep your business going, and if you're always trying to accelerate, you can easily spin out of control.

To avoid this risk, you have to embrace some humility and trust. Accept that you can't be responsible for everything. Then trust others to take some of the burden. Yes, this means it's time to delegate and develop your managerial skills. If you don't properly delegate, you not only place yourself at further risk of damaging your personal relationships; you also curtail the growth of your company and your employees. Building a great company takes a strong leader, after all, but a single person can only take that company so far. To reach the next level, it takes a *team*.

CHAPTER FIVE

Manage the External Forces

Stakeholders:

- ✓ You
- ✓ Your spouse
- ✓ Your children
- ✓ Your partners
- ✓ Your investor(s) or banker(s)
- ✓ Your employees
- ✓ Clients or customers
- ✓ Advisors and consultants
- ✓ Attorneys
- ✓ Your partner's partners
- ✓ Key management employees
- ✓ Board members
- ✓ Trustees

Emotions:

- Anxiety and confidence
- Security and greed
- Bad paranoia and good paranoia (good if it's used as a tool and controlled)
- Pride and too much pride
- Humility and too little humility
- Trust and vulnerability

Symptoms:

- Looking at key metrics to determine the efficiency of business operations
- Testing your limits more frequently vs. being comfortable and complacent
- A clear need to hire people to help fill the capacity gaps
- Anxiety about having to trust key aspects of the business to other people begins transitioning to contentment
- Instead of just keeping yourself motivated, you have to lead and motivate others
- New concepts emerge: management, goal setting, budgeting, outside consultants, and outsourcing
- Consistent refining and defining of your target market for your product or service (for the first time, you may have to say no to a customer, client, or vendor that doesn't fit the company mission, vision, or culture, not necessarily in that order)
- Debt and risk can be seen as opportunities, not liabilities
- People talk about you and your business as if you're a market leader

AT THIS POINT IN the Lifecycle, your biggest issue is probably cash management, not cash flow. But if you're not careful, you might get dangerously *comfortable* with your financial situation. This phase can cause you to switch from a mind-set of conserving cash to pay down debt to exactly the opposite. You begin to ask yourself, your partners, or your key employees, who are now stakeholders, questions like, "Should we take on debt or equity partners? Should we expand geographically or go into different product lines? Should we expand into a new plant or office space?"

These questions are challenging at any point in the Lifecycle, but they can be particularly daunting when they start to come up right at the moment when you finally have some cash flow to manage. You're just getting used to having some money on hand, and now your inner voice (and seemingly everyone else's) is asking you to spend it or even take on more debt.

Getting out of your comfort zone can be particularly valuable here, because around this time in the Entrepreneurial Lifecycle, you begin to accept a critical piece of wisdom (or if you haven't, then you'd better accept it soon): *You're either growing or you're dying.* Once you accept this premise, you will start to embrace how being in business is like sailing toward the horizon. As you near your goal, the horizon seems to keep moving further away. If you keep the right mind-set, this will just cause you to set new goals and keep sailing. But if you don't keep the right mind-set, you'll wind up extremely frustrated about how you never reach your goal. This is a sure way to go from growing to dying.

No matter which part of the Maturation Phase your business is in, you must remain committed to your mission. You must stay motivated. And as your team is now expanding, you must also continue to motivate them. This is a time when you have to lead, encourage, and keep a smile on your face (even as you grit your teeth about the obstacles and challenges that confront you in the organization and the outside market, no matter where you are in the Lifecycle). This is called *leadership*.

Breaking Through the Ceiling of Complexity

One clear sign that you're reaching Mid-Stage Growth is that you're becoming a market leader. Your capital is secure. Your personal financial survival is no longer an issue. Your customers are happy. Traction becomes momentum. This is when our old friends fear, anxiety, insecurity, and doubt pivot toward a whole new challenge: You begin to lose sleep over the question of how to find and retain the talent and capacity that will keep your business growing. Your main concern used to be money; now it's capacity. This is the point where you go beyond capital structure management and customer management and move on to *leadership* management so you can expand the company. Human capital is now the focus as opposed to financial capital.

Most great leaders eventually arrive at a key conclusion: It's possible to grow a business to a certain point on your own, but in order to break through the "ceiling of complexity," achieve continued growth, and expand to new heights, you must build a team and then place your trust in that team. The most successful leaders recognize this early in their journey.

Having to learn that you can't do it all can be challenging, but it's truly *excellent* news. Celebrate it. But then, as soon as you're done celebrating, start assessing your skills and limitations (your own and your company's) so you can identify the complementary talents and capacities your company needs to keep up with the market and grow at peak efficiency. If we pair this knowledge with what your industry is telling you, then we can identify a plan to effectively hire, delegate, and partner in ways that will take your company to the next level. In this chapter, we'll examine some strategies for doing exactly that.

Building an Effective Management Team

So, it's time to expand. But there is a difference between expanding effectively and expanding just for the sake of expanding. The difference is trust. As you begin adding new members and employees to your team, the key is to:

1. Hire people you are sure you can trust.
2. *Allow yourself* to fully trust their talents.
3. Give them the authority and autonomy to perform.

We all know that hiring is difficult. However, I have witnessed the toughest transition with numbers 2 and 3. Micromanagement and *nobody-can-do-it-better-than-me-itis* are symptoms I have seen many leaders exhibit, and those symptoms can severely limit a company's capabilities. Further, this condition invariably leads to morale deterioration and talent exodus. It is also bad for your health, marriage, and family life.

At this stage of Maturation, you have to trust and delegate. The first step is considering the emotional side of the coin. Trust requires humility. You must accept that your limitations aren't strictly limitations; they are opportunities to improve your company's capacity and performance.

One commonality among our most successful entrepreneur clients is the humility to give autonomous authority to others who have a talent to build departments, manage teams, lead divisions, and so on. I often say, "One of my best skills is hiring people smarter than me," and I have heard many others say the same thing. If you humbly and honestly assess your limitations, then you gain a clearer picture of the specific skill sets that can be complementary to yours in a way that will advance the mission of your emerging company.

Another invaluable exercise I learned from Dan Sullivan is called "Unique Ability." I brought this exercise home to Waldron Private Wealth, where I asked everyone on the leadership team to list all the tasks we performed in a day, week, and month and then categorize them into those that we believed 1) we were good at, 2) we were not good at, and 3) we felt we were the best at (those tasks that have highest impact on the organization): our unique ability. Then, as a group, we reviewed the lists to confirm these beliefs and have others challenge our self-evaluations. This was a vulnerable, humbling, and trust-building exercise.

If you commit to a similar exercise with your leadership team, what you will find is that your organization has many tasks and many people with skill sets complementary to each other. Knowing this information will allow you to take the critically important next step: Delegate all relevant tasks to the people who excel in the corresponding areas so that each leader can maximize the time they spend on them, and ensure the best use of their time and energy. In addition, all leadership team members will gain a greater appreciation of each other's skills and contributions. Ideally, once this occurs, you ensure that all company tasks are performed efficiently and effectively so the company will reach its highest potential. I personally instituted this concept in our company in 2006, and based on our company's financial metrics and industry financial performance, we have been in the top decile of performance in our industry ever since.

Delegating Comes in All Shapes and Sizes

Yes, proper delegation and trust can help break through the ceiling of complexity, but keep in mind that some ceilings are higher than others. Shattering some is a matter of telling people what to do. But for the higher ceilings, you have to build the *organization* to help you get there. If you've never read *Good to Great: Why Some Companies Make the Leap and Others Don't* by Jim Collins,[14] he has this excellent analogy

---

14 Jim Collins, *Good to Great: Why Some Companies Make the Leap . . . and Others Don't* (New York: HarperBusiness, 2011).

that compares organizations to a bus and their leaders to the bus driver. To paraphrase, the common belief is that the best bus drivers (leaders) will get behind the wheel and tell all their passengers (employees) where they're going to go. Then, he or she will simply start driving the bus. But the truth is that the best leaders recognize that the route is less important than the people on the bus. The goal needs to be to fill your bus with the *right* people with the *right* skills and place them in the *right* roles to keep your company moving in the right direction.

In this phase, it is all about assessing your people and getting the right ones in the right places. After you have committed to this process, the next step is to *trust* these people to guide your business on its journey. The humility to hire and delegate is key, because if you don't have that humility, then you will eventually peak as a business. You will limit your ability to grow beyond a certain point.

This is especially true because, as a company grows, it tends to endure two different periods of delegation. When you go from five to fifty employees, you're likely to still know every employee personally and will have firsthand knowledge and input on who each task and responsibility is being delegated to. But depending on the speed of your industry, you may also one day reach the point where you have to delegate from fifty to, say, 250 employees. In this case, you are unlikely to personally know every individual involved. You may have never met the person who needs to *hire* some of these new people. This kind of delegation requires a new level of trust. Now you have to trust the person who hires the people to get the job done. The challenge is making sure that your vision for the company supports the mission you originally established and that is understood and embraced by team members at all levels within your organization.

But what if you think everything is perfect? What if you believe that your team has all the skills you need and everyone is the right person in exactly the right role? This may be true for today, but a business at this stage is like a growing child: The clothes fit right now, but in three months, the kid will have outgrown them. Keep in mind that it's difficult to get outside your organization and view it objectively, particularly when you're at capacity limitation and you're focusing on fighting battles every day. Having an outside consultant assess your business for you frees you from this challenging task and also helps you see your limitations in an objective light. This opens you up to a willingness to accept advice on what needs to change and on a level most people can't reach on their own.

Make Agility Part of Your Culture

When we interview our clients about how they grew their businesses, they often reference times when they faced a turning point that changed their course completely. How they reacted to this turning point was usually the difference between them reaching the Transition Phase and floundering into mediocrity or failure. The leader that was insightful or lucky, or both, played a huge role in this correct decision, but let's not overlook another important quality of successful businesses: When the market changes or an obstacle presents itself, successful companies are usually agile enough to change quickly with a leadership team that demonstrates a high Velocity of Decision-Making.

Back in the summer of 2012, I had an aha moment that allowed me to break through the ceiling of my and my team's development. Three things were happening: 1) we had to completely restructure the compensation philosophy of all positions of the company to align with our industry and to where we had grown to as a company (a critical and emotionally charged task for all employee stakeholders); 2) due to our maturation and growth, we had to change our fundamental registration and regulatory investment operation, which then required us to change our key custody relationships (in other words, we tore our investment management operations down to the studs); and 3) I had a long-planned three-week family vacation to Europe that (at least in my own mind) was creating an artificial early deadline for us to meet numbers 1 and 2 above.

Fortunately, I had two tremendous team members—Mike Krol and Matt Helfrich, who have since become partners—helping me on two of these critical projects. I remember the day when I realized two things: Neither of the highly critical projects was going to be complete before I left for Europe, and my involvement in each project was limiting these team members' ability to execute the project management plan. These two fellows demonstrated excellent systematic project management skills to drive a complex, multifaceted project to defined goals, and I kept getting in their way. It was time for the second phase of delegation: delegating strategic planning.

I remember the exact moment this occurred to me. During a meeting with Mike, I noticed that I was anxiety ridden while he was sitting there calmly. I put down my pen and said, "You got this, don't you?"

"Oh yeah, absolutely," he said, calmly and confidently.

What happened next was liberating. Together, we defined what the project goals were—and we made sure they were SMART goals (specific, measurable, attainable, relevant, and timely). Once we had these, Mike walked me through the steps to be completed and outlined the progress report he would have for me when I returned from Europe. At that point, I could make my decisions and provide my input.

I left the meeting with Mike and walked down the hall to Matt's office. Matt was helping me (or should I say I was smothering Matt?) with the regulatory restructure. I asked him the same question: "You got this, don't you?"

His answer came with the same level of calm and confidence: "Absolutely!"

Because these two projects were critical and fundamental to the sustainability of our business, they emotionally shook every relationship we had. The regulatory change required us to move and alter every client engagement of the firm. Meanwhile, the compensation restructure to align with company goals, strategic plan, and industry standards moved the cheese of every employee in the firm. But the confidence Mike and Matt showed me, and the trust I placed in them, paid off in spades. I left for Europe without thinking about either project, and I was able to enjoy three memorable weeks with my family. Upon my return, each project plan was being meticulously executed. In fact, we were ahead of schedule. Both projects concluded within three months, and with exceptional results.

I was able to recognize that I needed to step back, delegate, and allow others to exercise their unique talents, which were complementary to mine and those of others. Since that summer, my role in the firm has evolved, and I am much happier and more productive. We now have a young and talented management and leadership team that spans beyond Matt and Mike. We matured and grew as an organization.

Emotional Lessons:

- Perform a self-evaluation. Take the time for you and each member of your team to be vulnerable and write down your strengths and weaknesses and be open to restructuring your role and responsibilities. Strong leaders are not afraid of this!
- People enjoy helping. For my business, and to enhance my own leadership, I turned to a mix of strategic inputs: 1) my brilliant clients; 2) leading industry colleagues from around the country (who were facing many of the same industry issues); and 3) a professional coach.
- Trust or die! Without trust, you cannot delegate. Without delegation, you cannot grow. If you are not growing, you are dying.

Technical Strategies:

- Hire for cultural fit. People are everything in business. Hire good talent when they are dislodged from their current situation and open for a change. But hire first for cultural fit.
- Give your employees permission to fail. Once you have become comfortable with delegating to others, the most important consideration is to train and mentor. *Then give them the permission to fail.* This is like teaching a child to ride a bicycle with training wheels. Eventually, you have to take the training wheels off and let go; otherwise, they never learn. I have seen great businesses lose great people or stagnate due to micromanagement and neutering management's effectiveness by usurping delegated authority. This is where your trust characteristic has to override. If you can do this, you will allow the individual's talents to flourish, and that will transcend into motivational behavior and the birth of a culture of trust and learning.
- Lead everyone else out of their comfort zone. The leader *and* everyone on the leadership team has to be forced to get out of their comfort zone. Figure out the catalyst for doing so in your business. As I have mentioned, I used an R&D budget that penalized management for not using it, and that sent a message to everyone on the team that we expect failure and are okay with it. If all experiments are a success, then they aren't experiments that involve risks and learning opportunities; they're *existing patterns.*
- If you want your business to outlast you, you have to delegate responsibility and accountability to the next generation of leaders in your organization.
- Understand the concept of Velocity of Decision-Making and be conscious of your work on it. The Velocity of Decision-Making is one of the best lessons I have learned from the great entrepreneurs and leaders I have had the privilege to work with. Those who have mastered this concept see advantages across the board. The velocity accelerates for

those who learn from and celebrate mistakes, embrace trust and delegate, and develop a great team that can effectively delegate execution.

It's a Collection of Efforts

As you gain traction and work to get it under control, you will realize that this is the birth of your business's identity. That identity is the collective efforts of you, your team, their personalities, and their passion. The heartbeat of this new entity is its culture. Like a newborn child, you now have to embrace your new responsibility of caring for its health, safety, and development in light of all the potential risks out there. It is no longer only about you. So as we move into the next chapter, let's think about expanding horizons—both for you and for your business.

CHAPTER SIX

Your Two Whys

Stakeholders:

- ⊘ You
- ⊘ Your spouse
- ⊘ Your children
- ⊘ Your partners
- ⊘ Your investor(s) or banker(s)
- ⊘ Your employees
- ⊘ Clients or customers
- ⊘ Advisors and consultants
- ⊘ Attorneys
- ⊘ Your partner's partners
- ⊘ Key management employees
- ⊘ Board members
- ⊘ Trustees

Emotions:

- ⊘ Fear that you will blow a really good thing
- ⊘ Anxiety related to letting go of things you used to control
- ⊘ Insecurity about this new territory and new role for yourself (the Peter Principle)
- ⊘ Pride for the entity that now has its own identity
- ⊘ Responsibility for all the families that depend on the company
- ⊘ Excitement about the discovery of what's next

Symptoms:

- ⊘ You have a new role, and your daily focus is different
- ⊘ Heightened sense of "company" instead of "self"
- ⊘ Fear-induced creative drive to keep the ship going in the right direction
- ⊘ Paranoia of not seeing the disruption "iceberg"
- ⊘ Desire to satisfy your stakeholders (and maybe investors) and provide career paths and opportunities for employees
- ⊘ Sudden capacity to work *on* your company instead of just *in* your company
- ⊘ Feelings of confliction, as you realize that you don't have all the answers but you think you should (take heart: not having all the answers is fine because you have a team to help you sail the ship)
- ⊘ The company has a different language, including terms like mission, vision, cultural fit, strategic plan, organic vs. inorganic growth, and so on

WHEN YOU STARTED THIS company, your central focus was to generate the results that would allow the company to survive, and ultimately, to grow. Now it is clear that you have momentum. Somewhere along the line—perhaps without you even realizing it—your day-to-day concerns evolved from keeping your company growing and improving to trying to define what your company means to you, your employees, your clients, your colleagues and competitors, and your community. You've gone from wondering *how* your company will exist to wondering *why* it exists (and will continue to exist after you have committed to Transition). In this chapter, we'll examine how some of the most successful entrepreneurs we have worked with over the years have arrived at the all-important answers to that question and how to find them for your company and for yourself.

There's a great book by Rich Karlgaard called *The Soft Edge: Where Great Companies Find Lasting Success.*[15] These concepts are definitely what Karlgaard would refer to as "soft edge," as they are related to the culture, values, and Emotional Intelligence that hold most great companies together. The soft-edge concepts aren't usually something that a company is founded on. Most entrepreneurs don't start their company saying, "This is our culture." It usually isn't until sometime during the Maturation Phase that business owners begin to articulate a company culture that is personified both by themselves and by the team they have built around them.

Admittedly, these were difficult pieces for me to define early on. Like many other entrepreneurs, I spent my Survival Phase with my head down, driving through what needed to be done. The same was true for much of our company's Maturation Phase (which we're still enjoying presently). For a long while, it felt like we didn't have time for these softer issues. But then I reached the point where I finally had the desire and capacity to work *on* our company as opposed to *in* it.

With their actions, passionate leaders personify their mission and vision and, without even being aware, inspire others to follow them. Their actions become the mission statement. They don't even have to write it down. As companies grow, eventually most leaders get to the

---

15 Rich Karlgaard, *The Soft Edge: Where Great Companies Find Lasting Success* (Hoboken, NJ: Jossey-Bass, 2014).

point where they formally define their mission and vision, but the best companies and leaders define and live their *why* as early in the Lifecycle as possible.

The Two *Why*s: Organizational and Personal

One of the most famous and widely viewed Ted Talks is Simon Sinek's brilliant *How Great Leaders Inspire Action*.[16] The central message is that most companies know *what* they do and some know *how* they do it, but only the best companies know the answer to *why* they do it. "People don't buy what you do," he says. "They buy *why* you do it." To highlight the message, he compares Apple products to those offered by other consumer electronics companies, pointing out that the reason Apple is so effective and has developed a dedicated, long-lasting, and massive customer base is because they always frame their pitch and purpose with *why*. When you think Apple, you think about what they *stand for* as much as you think about what their products look like and do.

Starting with *why* is the difference between focusing your pitch with the facts and figures behind what makes your product or service great and imparting a lasting message about your company's central purpose. If you highlight the *why* over the *what* and *how*, your company will not only align with greater potential for success, but it will also develop a more dedicated following from the people who value its purpose, which will set it up for more sustained growth.

In other words, your *why* creates the emotional bond and experience (versus a transaction) with your customers, vendors, and employees. If you don't impart the emotional connection through your definition of the reason why you exist, then you are at high risk of being commoditized. A cup of coffee is just that: ground coffee beans

---

16 Simon Sinek, "How Great Leaders Inspire Action," TED Talk, https://www.ted.com/talks/simon_sinek_how_great_leaders_inspire_action?language=en.

steeped in water. But because they have defined their why, Starbucks is an emotional experience.

From your *why* flows your mission and vision statements, and all of these components drive your underlying company culture. It's an incredibly powerful message—one that works for any company, no matter what they do or where they find themselves on the Entrepreneurial Lifecycle.

I did not start my company with a full awareness of its why. Some entrepreneurs do, but most don't. I plowed forward through Survival just trying to keep my head above water. When questioning our clients who own businesses, we found that most figured out their why in early maturity but wished they had been able to identify it even earlier. The earlier the better, but better late than never.

When I first encountered this eye-opening concept, it made me reflect not only on what our company stood for but also on my personal experience and the experience of all those other entrepreneurs our company has worked with over the years. It occurred to me that while a company might have one central *why*, the entrepreneurs who lead them have two. The first is the *why* of the organization—everything that defines the mission, the culture, and the purpose. The other is the *why* of the entrepreneur, or all the personal reasons he or she established this business and what he or she wants to get out of it.

Both of these *why*s drive the company and its leader through the Maturation Phase, and both of them influence big decisions and bring about difficult emotions as you move toward Transition. The organizational *why* is what will keep your company growing both now and after you're no longer running it. The personal *why* will go a long way to informing what you hope to get out of the Transition Phase and what you will do with your life after the company is in someone else's hands.

The Organizational *Why*: Your Culture, Your Purpose

The fun part in the Maturation Phase is when you get to experience your momentum shift to acceleration, and sometimes it feels unstoppable. As you are experiencing this growth and adding more people, the other thing that is happening (often unintentionally and without your realizing) is that the values and culture of the business are starting to form. You're bringing in other employees and new team members, promoting new managers, and adding all these new perspectives to the mix—or as Jim Collins puts it, you're bringing people on the bus.[17]

Your culture is driven by your organizational *why*. But how do you define it, especially in the early stages of the Lifecycle? It helps to start simple and then build outward.

At Waldron Private Wealth, we went about it backward. We started with what we thought was a complete definition of our *why*, but we soon learned that we needed to add more to the story. Late in our Survival Phase, we were introduced to a potential new client whose business would accelerate our momentum. The client was a widow whose husband, an executive at a public company, had recently passed away. In an effort to demonstrate our unique services, we poured quite a few hours into showing her the value we could bring, and we did it all on our dime. We were thrilled that we were able to help this woman in so many ways, and that we were retained.

Six months into a deepening relationship, I received a call from our client's brother. He made it clear in no uncertain terms that he didn't understand the value we were providing and the effort we were putting in. I did what I could to educate him on the issues his sister was facing. However, I soon realized that our conversation wasn't *logical*, but rather,

---

17 Jim Collins, *Good to Great: Why Some Companies Make the Leap . . . and Others Don't* (New York: HarperBusiness, 2011).

emotional. He was too entrenched emotionally to learn the facts and benefits of our advice, and therefore, he resorted to challenging our integrity.

To show him that we would never jeopardize our integrity, no matter
the price, I refunded the entire fee from day one, even though we knew
the client was experiencing the benefits of our *why*. I took the gun out
of his hand. He was a little shocked that I did that, and the tone of the
conversation changed completely. In that moment, I defined a central
part of our company's *why*, which has become a bedrock of our culture:
Our integrity is priceless. From that day forward, our entire organization understood that our reputation and our clients' satisfaction would
always be more important than money. This act demonstrated the *why*
more clearly than any training or tagline could. It provided an illus-
tration of our value proposition, one that all current and future team
members could buy into. Our culture was born.

And as an aside, the brother and I developed a respectful relationship
based on this situation. He eventually understood our value and has
referred several clients to us.

Based on this experience, we went back and redefined our organizational *why* by starting with the simplest definition: We are in the
business of helping people. That's our central and simplified *why*. If we
break it down to this, we justify most of our actions by attempting to
help people however we can: the weekend call from a business owner
who lost her job via the new owners of her business post-sale, the late-
night call from a widow who recently lost her husband, the early-morn-
ing call from a parent whose child is suffering from addiction issues.
Quite simply, we're in business to help.

From that foundation, we were able to identify the fuller definition of our organizational *why*:

THE WHY BEHIND WALDRON

WE STRIVE TO SIMPLIFY THE LIVES OF INDIVIDUALS AND THEIR FAMILIES, AND TO ELIMINATE THE STRESS AND ANXIETY CREATED BY THE COMPLEXITIES OF WEALTH. WE WORK TO ENHANCE THE QUALITY OF OUR CLIENTS' LIVES, ALLOWING THEM TO SPEND MORE TIME DOING WHAT BRINGS THEM JOY AND HAPPINESS. WE SIMPLIFY THE COMPLEXITIES OF WEALTH, TO GIVE THEM BACK THE MOST PRECIOUS COMMODITY OF ALL: TIME!

In addition to the mission statement above, we have defined our cultural pillars as follows:

- Be entrepreneurial and creative
- Be collaborative
- Exhibit integrity in everything we do
- We are Driven to Make a Difference (DTMAD)
- Tie every action and decision we make back to simplifying life for our clients

Based on these cultural pillars, we now have a deeper understanding of *how* we can serve our clients in a way that meets our organizational *why*. To this day, before we proceed with any client relationship, we make sure that there is no misunderstanding about our purpose or approach to service and that both parties are confident that we can add value to their situation. We give our prospective clients the ability to evaluate us by investing thirty to fifty hours of our professional time to make sure we are an absolute right fit for their unique situation. When we take prospects through our GAP process (gather, analyze, and present), we are interviewing them every bit as much as they are interviewing us. We ask, "Can we deliver, and can they receive our *why* experience?"

Our client relationships are long term and typically operate across two or even three generations. Knowing this, it is critically important that we feel confident that we can deliver our promised experience to the clients' situation by helping them achieve their personal and financial goals while eliminating the stress and anxiety that naturally comes with increased wealth. We would rather say no to a client who isn't the right fit (either for our reasons or theirs) than take on someone who won't work well with us. Doing so would be damaging to our culture.

Your Organizational *Why* Is Always Evolving

There is great benefit in focusing on values over capital, especially during the Maturation and Transition Phases. You have to understand the importance of being intentional about your culture and values. At our company, we take this point so seriously that we have a Culture Committee whose purpose it is to ensure that our culture and values are translating properly to all team members and that it evolves appropriately as the company grows. This committee works to unite the team, establishes service projects in the community, composes a regular newsletter that keeps our entire staff informed and highlights overachievement, and finally, they promote *fun*.

One of our culture committee's biggest projects was to spend essentially all of 2017 defining our company's culture. My son Shea began the process by interviewing the executive team and other key players within the company in search of the answer to an important question: What makes Waldron Private Wealth different? From these many hours of interviews, the culture committee boiled down the response to the notion that we always strive to make a difference, we are collaborative in everything we do, and we are driven by an entrepreneurial spirit.

Around this same time, we were engaging with a construction project—a beautiful new building for our organization. We made the decision that we would include in the design a series of four walls that represent what our company stands for. The first wall is the one our people and visitors see when they step off the elevator. Offset with the company name is an art installation featuring an intricate network of strings (meant to represent that life and wealth are complex) that have been redirected to form our tagline, "Simplifying wealth. Simplifying life." This speaks to our central value proposition that by hiring us, you're simplifying your wealth *and* your life.

The second wall stands behind our main reception desk. The wall features a photo of a geode (meant to represent the passage of time and the preservation of value), along with the statement, "The most precious commodity is time."

Just across from this piece is our "Waldron by the Numbers" wall. On this wall, a row of vertical bars holds a series of rotating panels. On one side of each panel is a number, and on the other side is the event or milestone to which the number corresponds. Alongside numbers like clients under management, we proudly display more personal numbers like babies born to the staff, hours of community service we have performed in the past year, and the number of homes we have helped our clients buy.

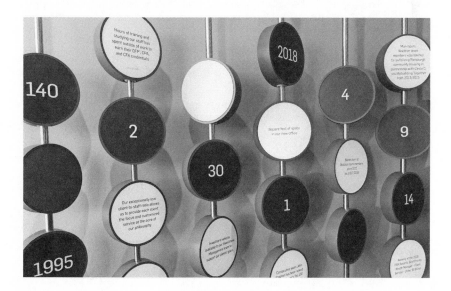

The final wall is the one dearest to us: our culture wall. This installation features a photo of every member of the team interspersed with sections of our mission statement. It highlights the most valuable asset we have and who it is that delivers value to our clients every day: our team.

However you approach your own organizational *why*, it is important to broadcast that *why* wherever and however you can. Having these culture walls has helped us keep our culture top of mind for our team members, but just as importantly, it has left a positive impression with everyone who has visited our office.

The bigger picture is that—ideally at least—this all becomes a numbers game. As your company grows, you take on more and more employees. This is wonderful, but from an organizational *why* perspective, you have to keep in mind that the bigger your company gets, the further the next employee gets from the stories that defined what your business is today. That's why our company focuses on providing our value proposition formally to our employees at least once every year. For the benefit of new employees, we tell the story of how our business came to be and explain how our company's heritage helps define its culture. This ensures that everyone remains connected to our organizational *why*, no matter how big the company gets.

Similarly, it's important to keep in mind that your organization's *why* is a living organism that needs to be tended and fed, or your culture either dies or becomes something unintentional. Treat culture like you treat your children. If you want it to grow up right, you have to pay attention to it, nurture it, and correct it when it gets off track.

If you recognize that your culture is always evolving and growing, you position yourself for opportunities to improve as an organization that you might not have seen otherwise. For instance, we recently made a huge investment in a new building entirely because we saw it as an opportunity to communicate how much we value our employees' comfort and well-being. I was skeptical at first about what our design consultants and architects were telling us about how this would transform our business.

Our developer, Jim Scalo, coached me on how office space is an investment in people and culture as opposed to just "space." For insight into this organizational investment, see his book *Work Them to Life: Upgrade Your Office Space to Win the Talent War*.[18] After we moved in, I was blown away by how the space became such an integral part of culture.

This is the value of focusing on the growth and evolution of your organizational *why*: When you do, you learn new ways to supplement the good work that your people are doing. You keep your culture evolving and improving as your company evolves and improves. Instead of thinking about the space you rent as an expense, think about your space as an asset that enhances everything your company does.

The Personal Why: *Things* versus *Experience*

Once you have identified the *why* of your organization, it is time to turn the question inward. Identifying your personal *why* is usually a matter of answering the question of what you want to get out of this business or out of life after the business. Sure, money is a big factor, but money and wealth are only the surface-level answers. If you guide your company to the end of the Maturation Phase and into Transition, you probably won't ever have to worry about money again. To ensure that your company continues its success after you're done running it—and to ensure that you lead the best quality life when you leave the company—you have to understand so much more than just the money.

I know exactly where I was when I identified this condition and connected it to its antidote, which is identifying your personal *why*. I was on a plane to New York and reading an article which noted that there are things and experiences that consume our time and resources. Some people appreciate and enjoy things like cars, houses, clothing, jewelry, and other rare collectibles. Some people like spending their time and

---

18 Jim Scalo, *Work Them to Life: Upgrade Your Office Space to Win the Talent War* (Pittsburgh: Burns Scalo Development, 2018).

resources on life experiences. There is no right or wrong answer, only what the individual enjoys in life. And they are not mutually exclusive. Some like an equal helping of both.

The article went on to explain that each of us prioritizes *things* and *experiences* differently. The way *things* and *experiences* impact our lives are specific to the individual. It hit me like a ton of bricks: Maureen and I clearly prioritize life experiences over things. At the same time, given that our company counsels many wealthy entrepreneurs, I have seen a host of different ways that people balance their own personal *why*. Some of our clients engage with some incredibly interesting life experiences, while others value cool and unique things.

- *Things:* Some collect cars, rare coins, or watches, and we have one client who collects rare fountain pens. Other clients collect additional businesses via minority investments because, quite frankly, their hobby has morphed into running or helping to run businesses.
- *Experiences:* Some enjoy the experience of teaching or mentoring, others travel to experience different cultures, and many volunteer at their church or a homeless shelter. One client has a mission to see a baseball game in every city. And another is doing the same in every National Hockey League arena.
- *Combo:* Some collect unique houses in cool locations so they can spend quality time with family and friends.

At Waldron Private Wealth, we have a process that helps each of our clients and their families understand their own priorities and balance between *experiences* and *things*. And it is remarkable how the balance can change over time. Many of our clients are very much into *things* at the start of their Maturation Phase and then move toward valuing *experiences* as they approach and move through Transition. But eventually, everyone prioritizes the value of quality time. This is part of why our geode wall in the lobby of our building gets such a positive reaction. Time is such a valuable commodity, and the best way to get more of it as you move into the later phases of the Lifecycle and accumulate more wealth is to simplify your life. This can be an experience in itself. Simplifying your life involves eliminating the unnecessary clutter in life and having a process and trusted team to help simplify how you deal with anything that can't be eliminated.

In almost every situation I have been involved with, this discovery of the personal *why* eventually culminates in the emotion of gratitude and a desire to give back. This move is high up the priority list during the Transition Phase, so we'll discuss more about giving back and family philanthropic pursuits in the chapters to come.

Emotional Lessons:

- Get introspective. Dig deep into your self-awareness of your organizational *why* and personal *why*. Your family members, employees, customers, vendors, and other stakeholders add gravity to this sense of purpose. Find both *why*s, and you will inspire yourself and those around you.
- Accept your multiple personalities! As CEO and owner, you have two different roles. Be aware of the different emotional drivers of each role.
- Understand that as you advance through this phase, your other interests will start to creep into your mind more often. What is it that inspires you—things, experiences, or a combination of the two? There is no right answer, but knowing that answer will become incredibly important as you move toward Transition.

Technical Strategies:

- Culture is key. Define it and nurture it. It is rooted in your *why*.

Your Whys Must Continue to Align

The earlier you know your *whys*, the more growth your company will enjoy during Maturation and the more *you* will enjoy the experience. When you are aware of your two *whys*, it becomes easier to see when they are no longer working in unison (which is a clear symptom that it's time to Transition). A key step in our wealth management process is helping our clients identify these two dynamics. Without a clear picture of why they are doing things, we can't help them define their goals or advise how to get there. Often, we have to go through a tough and sensitive line of questioning to unearth the *real* reason a decision (or no decision) is being made.

A client of ours summarized it well: "I wear two hats—one as an owner and one as CEO—and oftentimes, they're in conflict with each other on critical strategy decisions." This client was at the point where he was considering a transition of some or all of his company and felt himself taking more conservative positions when discussing how to grow and take advantage of his company's industry and market leadership. He realized that his personal desires and risk tolerance as owner were negatively affecting his decision-making as CEO. When you experience this kind of conflict, it might be time to consider stepping back so you can take a broader view of why your company exists and why (or why not) you are still the person to run it.

This is an introspective process for most. If you have done a good job of self-reflection, you have created a new, highly effective leadership team and delegated authority. This frees your mind to look at the broader vision for the company and yourself. Now, as you approach the Transition Phase of growth, you will find yourself at another fork in the road. Do you sell or transition leadership to the next generation, or do you scale up and face the next challenge? To find the answer, you must first ask if your *whys* are still aligned.

Transition

CHAPTER SEVEN

Transition, Sale, or Succession

Stakeholders:

- ✓ You
- ✓ Your spouse
- ✓ Your children and their spouses
- ✓ Your grandchildren and maybe their spouses
- ✓ Your partner(s)
- ✓ Your investors or bankers
- ✓ The management team
- ✓ Your employees
- ✓ Board members
- ✓ Ex-spouse(s)
- ✓ Stepchildren
- ✓ Partner(s) spouses
- ✓ Partner(s) heirs
- ✓ Trustee(s)
- ✓ Partner(s) trustee(s)
- ✓ Any and every stakeholder's attorney(s)

Emotions:

- Fear about many different aspects and potential pitfalls related to succession planning
- Love and its frequent counterpart: conflict
- Responsibility to those who stand to gain from this business in the future
- Insecurity that if the plan isn't perfect, your business won't succeed after you're no longer running it
- Anxiety about the prospect of doing new things in life
- Power vs. freedom—the power you have to control your business, the power you stand to lose when you're no longer in charge, and the power to dole out responsibilities and rewards to the next generation of your business and family
- Fear of losing your identity as the founding leader of the company, and loneliness when you lose structured daily interaction

Symptoms:

- When you start to feel like you don't have the energy or the skill set to take your business to the next level, it's time to think about transition.
- You feel anxious about the responsibility you have to all your stakeholders and your stewardship of the value that your business has created.
- The fear you've carried throughout the Lifecycle shifts from survival to loss of opportunity and then to a sense that you need to find the perfect person or people to take over for you before the business declines.
- You might find yourself behaving more defensively than offensively.
- Your goals and aspirations are changing.

WHENEVER CLIENTS ASK US when they should start succession planning, the answer is always the same: As soon as you can. There is no exact moment in the Entrepreneurial Lifecycle that we can point to as the best moment, except to say that it's time to start succession planning as soon as you have something to pass on. Unfortunately, it's often the case (and I can vouch for this personally) that you don't realize you have enterprise value until you're already into the Maturation Phase. Up to that point, you're simply trying to get sustained cash flow to meet obligations and then have some cash for yourself. Then, when you do, you have earnings to multiply by a multiple, which equals *enterprise value*. "Voila!" you say. "Look what I found!" At this point, you are building a personal balance sheet. Part of that balance sheet is the business (or the goose that is laying the golden eggs).

So that's the good news. The slightly less good news is that guiding a business through its growth period can be a stressful and time-consuming process. So is succession planning. The prospect of doing both at the same time might sound daunting. But keep in mind that succession planning is absolutely essential. It's one of those things that success adds to your to-do list. The longer you go without it, and the larger your enterprise and its value becomes, the more risk you take on. It's like driving without insurance. From this day forward, personal wealth management, business planning, and family governance are inextricably tied together.

Once you comprehend the risk of not prioritizing succession planning, you start to think about the responsibility you have to all stakeholders, from family to ex-family to employees. Speaking of your stakeholders, you might have noticed that the list at the beginning of each chapter is getting longer. There's good reason for this: As you move through the phases and your business grows, there are many people who have an interest in your business and its transition. With so many people involved, both the technical and emotional picture gets incredibly complicated. This is why timing is so important, as is integration, communication, and education.

Now that we've established these points, let's discuss what this chapter *isn't*. It *isn't* a definitive guide to succession planning. While I will outline a more macro approach to succession planning and discuss what knowledge and materials you will need if you hope to be optimally prepared, what I *won't* do is delve into what-ifs—all those specific complexities about how to keep every heir satisfied, or how to manage situations where people you count on aren't as interested in running the business as you thought they might be, or what to do when one heir wants to run the business but isn't nearly as capable as another heir who is less interested in taking over, and the list goes on and on. Every business, every family, every group of stakeholders is unique, and so every individual succession plan must also be unique. This makes it impossible for us to cover every potential scenario that you might encounter.

What we can do is take a 20,000-foot view of the key questions to ask and answer before you retain a professional who can help you put together a successful succession plan.

Integrate, Communicate, and Educate

In the next twenty-five years, $68 trillion dollars in wealth will pass from one generation to the next.[19] When considering transferring your own portion of that fortune, you will need to contend with many technical strategies related to business operational management and control, tax efficiency, and trust and estate planning. These planning issues then have to be coordinated with the human, family side. In the past five to ten years, we have noticed a change in most clients' goals and priorities.

19 MacKenzie Sigalos, "$68 Trillion is about to Change Hands in the US," CNBC, November 20, 2018.

More people are trending toward the softer, human side over the hard, technical planning issues. Specifically, there is a greater emphasis on how to integrate, communicate, and educate the next generation about business succession and wealth management.

Seven years ago, in reaction to this increasingly common client request, Waldron Private Wealth designed a service offering to address exactly these issues, including investing in training younger advisors who are contemporaries of the next generation. We created our Next Generation Wealth Planning and Education services. This is becoming a hot item for people, mostly because:

- America is aging, and the demographic shift is leading to the large impending wealth transfer I mentioned at the start of this section.
- The senior generation understands that matters of wealth are unique to every family.
- There are many dangers associated with getting the message wrong and failing to integrate, communicate, and educate correctly.
- Colleges and universities do not do a good job of providing graduates with basic, let alone advanced, wealth management skills and concepts.

By integrating education and communication across all generations, we help our clients arrive at more comprehensive succession planning strategies designed to keep *all* stakeholders satisfied. Our advice is often-times more psychological than technical or financial in nature. Succession planning is particularly personal and emotional. It takes time to develop, requires constant attention and nurturing, and its foundation is education and *open and honest* communication.

Common Questions

In furtherance of educating and communicating, let's examine the most common questions about succession planning, starting with the most obvious:

WHAT IS SUCCESSION PLANNING?

Succession planning is the plan for orderly transition of management or ownership of a business and wealth over time. It's the plan you follow when the time has come to turn the leadership of your business over to the next team of leaders and owners. The earlier you start planning, the more time you spend on that plan, and the more often you update it, the higher its probability of success. Unfortunately, there are situations where, due to sudden and unforeseen circumstances like death, illness, or disability, time is not always a luxury you can afford.

The plan has to be written and developed for any and all potential future leaders—and this includes key stakeholders like partners, managers, and your children, even if those children are in high school (or even in *diapers*) when you begin planning. It must provide for dealing with equally loved children who may have similar desires, skills, and ambitions. Or worse yet, it might have to provide for children who have equal ambitions and different skills and drives, children who might also have spouses chirping in their ears and pointing out why they are more *entitled* to wealth and control than their sibling(s). And let's not forget that this plan then has to be coordinated with the estate planning strategy of the senior generation and the estate tax system. The complexities can make for a very challenging process.

As you can imagine, this tends to be one of the most emotionally charged planning matters that you will face during the Entrepreneurial Lifecycle. What could possibly go wrong?

WHEN SHOULD I START THINKING ABOUT SUCCESSION PLANNING?

We hear this question often because sometimes it's difficult to find the time, particularly when you're in the middle to late stages of the Maturation Phase. Succession planning is typically a daunting parallel demand for entrepreneurs and business leaders. It takes skill, discipline, and at the same time, patience—and during this most trying of phases, all of those qualities are likely to be stretched a little thin.

When you're in a hot industry segment, succession planning is more about business management and capital optimization. In this situation, you're addressing management of capacity limitation brought on by exponential growth. While facing deadlines, expanding capacity demands, and investigating estate planning opportunities, an entrepreneur can feel like he or she is being pulled in any number of directions at once. When you're up to your eyeballs in decisions related to raising capital so you can keep growth at the forefront, how are you supposed to dedicate any energy or attention to the most complex, forward-looking aspect of the Entrepreneurial Lifecycle?

In our experience at Waldron Private Wealth, we have noticed that most entrepreneurs share two commonalities related to *when* they start thinking about succession planning:

1. They begin to think about succession planning when they have reached the point where they have begun to delegate, and management responsibilities have been disseminated among the team. This allows the founder(s) to have the bandwidth for new priorities (like succession planning).

2. Founding owners tend to start thinking about succession planning between the ages of fifty and fifty-five. While we mention this topic to our entrepreneur clients early and often, most of them don't genuinely start to think about it until

they realize they are looking toward the next chapter in their lives. When that AARP application first arrives, they reconcile with their own mortality for the first time, and then they start wondering about how to ensure the best life for their children (who are becoming young adults) and thinking about other interests they would like to pursue after the business transitions to the next generation.

As an addendum, in the scenarios where the entrepreneur is a member of the second generation of the business, he or she will tend to think about the succession plan with more frequency. This is for one of two reasons: Either they have been living the plan since long before they even took control, or they are now leading a business *without* a succession plan from the senior generation, and they're dealing with the associated chaos that comes with being put in that position.

Whatever your situation, make no mistake that the time to think about succession planning is *as soon as you have something valuable to pass on.* Even if you're not an AARP member and your heirs are still toddlers, it is important to identify and codify everything that you want to happen when it's time to sell or transition your company to the next generation. Conversely, the time to *stop* thinking about your succession plan is *never.* The best succession plans aren't "set it and forget it"—they must change and evolve as businesses change and evolve and stakeholders grow and change. Succession planning is not a task; it's an ongoing, dynamic process.

WHAT SHOULD I BE MOST CONCERNED ABOUT WHEN I START WORKING ON MY SUCCESSION PLAN?

Good succession plans focus on successor management, ownership transfer, and wealth transfer. How do I involve the next generation (both family and other stakeholders) in the control of the business, and how do I ensure that the wealth passes to them in a way that makes sense for everyone?

If you have done the succession planning legwork, then you have identified emerging talent in the company, mentored them, and prepared them for leadership roles as an ongoing part of the company's growth. This helps your business be in a better position to successfully transition after a founder or CEO steps down or otherwise passes on ownership. On the wealth side, the legwork calls for open and honest communication with the family, working to achieve the family vision, identifying how to engage and integrate everyone, avoiding hurting anyone's feelings (this only comes with expectation setting), and keeping the family together. With time and consistent communication and education, an individual heir's expectations have a better chance of aligning with reality.

As I mentioned earlier, every succession plan is unique. There is no one-size-fits-all, step-by-step procedure to ensure that you are doing it correctly. So the short answer is that the best succession plans are the most thorough. We have all seen the statistics: Approximately 66 percent of businesses fail in the second generation, and an estimated 85 percent fail when passed to the third generation—this in spite of a lot of smart people studying and advising on the subject.[20] The reason for this high failure rate is lack of consistent attention to this critical planning matter. Succession planning is extremely difficult, as most extremely important things are.

---

20 Aileron, "The Facts of Family Business," *Forbes*, July 31, 2013, https://www.forbes.com/sites/aileron/2013/07/31/the-facts-of-family-business/#100f174f9884.

WHAT ARE SOME OF THE QUESTIONS I SHOULD ANSWER TO HELP SUPPORT MY SUCCESSION PLAN?

Again, the best succession plans are the most thorough, so there are dozens of key questions to ponder as the planning begins. Here is a list of ten of them, for starters:

1. How many owners or partners are involved in the business, and are any of them a controlling partner?
2. Who are the people you can identify as potentially serving in the next generation of leadership?
3. How many children do I have, and do any of them have the desire or possess the skill set to run the business?
4. Is the capital structure conducive to succession?
5. Should I consider sharing any portion of ownership while I'm still running the business? If so, what are the terms the other party(ies) needs to meet to secure their percentage of ownership?
6. Will I transition the business outright or in a trust?
7. If I'm passing this on to my children, will it be a sale or a gift? Under what terms?
8. If any of my heirs are minors when the transition happens, will they require special business trustees? And if so, when can those trustees be recused?
9. How will we manage to control governance among the family or management team? Will we need to establish voting blocs for different families involved with the company? How about voting trusts?
10. What is the policy on spouses? Can they be employed at the company? Can they attend meetings? Are prenups required so ownership is controlled only by lineal heirs?

Yes, succession planning is extremely complicated. And these are just *ten* of the questions that can intimidate and cause a business leader to procrastinate.

Communication and Transparency

Many years ago, we helped the four children of a client work through their issues with co-ownership of their mother's business after she passed. At some point during the succession planning process, their mother had decided that the best way for the business to be run in the next generation would be for one of her children to assume total control. Her fear was that if she spread control evenly, it would lead to disputes between the siblings and would likely slow the Velocity of Decision-Making necessary to keep the company thriving. So she chose one of her children—the one she believed best equipped to run the company—and irrevocably granted him full control over the operating agreement and the business, in all aspects. All four children received equal share ownership, but total control went to one of them.

This second-generation leader took that control gratefully. However, the mother did not communicate the plan during her life, nor did she hold stakeholder meetings to educate the heirs on how she would like the governance handled. Transparency was not part of the culture (as an aside, we see this trend changing in late-stage boomers, Generation Xers, and certainly in millennials). The son wasn't trained in, nor particularly concerned with, communication or transparency with his equal-share partners. This proved costly, as communication and transparency must remain at the core of everything you do in business, but particularly during the challenging Transition Phase.

What followed was the classic example of what happens when one is not trained on what to do with the power of control. Greed crept into the picture. You would never allow a child to sail a ship out into the ocean without careful and prolonged training. This situation was just as dangerous. The relationships deteriorated to the point where the other three shareholders experienced erratic distributions and minimal communication as the controlling shareholder seemed to be enjoying a grander lifestyle. Without communication and transparency, this left the other siblings to the demons of their imagination.

The fallout from the frequent arguments about money and control led the family to begin aligning into factions. Animosity soared, family get-togethers became less frequent (and more awkward than ever before), and interaction between the siblings ran cold at best and contentious at worst. Waldron Private Wealth entered the picture as a mediator to try to mend the relations, improve transparency, and increase the consistency of distributions. This worked for a little while, but sadly, the process concluded with a contentious buyout by the controlling shareholder. The siblings no longer speak to each other.

This example highlights the importance of consistent communication by the senior generation (God willing and time permitting) with the next generation, teaching them how to manage the business, and more importantly, educating them on the importance of communication and transparency as a responsibility of the governing person or body. The other lesson that this example teaches is the importance of providing governance provisions that allow for a broader voice or mechanism to prevent the ugly emotions of power, greed, control, dominance, and jealousy from running wild.

Timing and Flexibility

So, the time to start planning—particularly if you're wondering whether your children have the interest or capacity to take over for you after the transition—is now (or better yet, *yesterday*). The sooner you start outlining the details, the more you can involve your children or successor(s) in the plan itself. Not only does having a plan in place help ensure that your next-generation leaders are more knowledgeable and better equipped to run your business when the time comes, it also covers you in the event of tragedy.

Because tragedy can strike at any time, there is nothing more damaging than procrastination to estate and succession planning. On several occasions, we have witnessed entrepreneurs who have unfortunately become disabled or passed away before fully implementing (and on many occasions, even *starting*) their estate and succession plan.

One of the stories I followed early in my career as a young accountant in the Miami office of a major accounting firm was that of Joe Robbie, the former owner of the Miami Dolphins and Joe Robbie Stadium. For years, the team at this accounting firm had been urging Mr. Robbie to engage in estate planning to provide liquidity for estate taxes in the event of his death. Approximately six years after I left Miami to start Waldron Private Wealth, I read on the front page of *USA Today* that the Robbie family estate had sold the Dolphins to Wayne Huizenga for fifty cents on the dollar so they could pay a $47 million estate tax bill following Mr. Robbie's untimely death (as if death is ever timely).

Now, even if your business isn't worth quite as much as an NFL franchise, not having a detailed succession and estate plan can leave it without a management succession strategy in place. Of course infighting will ensue. In some cases, the wrong person will wind up being installed as the next-generation leader, and as a result, customers, vendors, and employees all suffer. On top of this, this kind of upheaval can create tremendous discord within the family, loss of tenured talent among the staff, and threats to the potential health of the company and therefore its enterprise value.

But just as important as timing is the matter of flexibility. This is because nothing in business or in life ever exists in a vacuum. When you first begin your planning process, your children or successor(s) will have certain interests, skill sets, and qualities—all of which are bound to evolve and change over time. Further, their lives will change as they get married, move into new houses, have children, and gain or lose interest in certain careers.

This is exactly why you must provide for flexibility. Often the succession plan is being put in place when the children are toddlers, decades before they're ready to begin their careers, let alone take over a business. Over the course of those decades, those children might grow into exactly the kind of leader your business needs. Or they might not. Either way, your stakeholders will change. Your goals and desires will change. You might find yourself no longer wanting to be in the business, and quite a bit sooner than you anticipated. Or your business suddenly may have a need for different skill sets to avoid becoming obsolete. If you have too much rigidity in your succession plan, it could lead to problems.

Your Two Hats

Furthering the complexities of succession planning is the fact that there are two different but related efforts that you must undertake as the senior-generation leader. Recall the quote from a client of ours: "I wear two hats—one as an owner and one as CEO, and oftentimes, they're in conflict with each other on critical strategy decisions."

The first effort is called *succession leadership*. This is what we discussed in previous chapters when we outlined the need for delegation of tasks, development of management talent, and delegation of authority. This is the building out of the organizational chart that will make the current business both sustainable and forward-thinking in terms of where the industry and the business is going. Succession management is mandatory if you intend to build enterprise value. Only with a mature organizational chart structured to support growth and a deep management team to execute strategy can a business reach its full potential of value creation.

The second effort, *succession ownership*, is quite different from the first. Succession ownership can mean different things to different people, and it tends to have radically different structures and paths that depend on multiple factors. One of the most critical factors is the industry of the business. Currently, Waldron Private Wealth is working with three entrepreneurs in high-growth sectors, which means that, in their case, succession ownership is about monetizing a substantial minority or a substantial majority to private equity. The reasons range from needing access to capital and talent at an exponential rate that requires a private equity or strategic partner to the realization that the velocity of growth and decision-making has exceeded their capabilities.

Shares and Heirs

As I indicated earlier, succession planning is a long and continuous process. Think of it like a sculpture: You start with a vision, and then you mold it and shape it over time until that vision comes into focus. If you're hoping to pass your business on to the next generation of your family, then there are three key parallel tracks to follow as you prepare those leaders to take over for you:

1. Prepare the *shares*.
2. Prepare the *business*.
3. Prepare the *heirs*.

Every great succession plan—particularly in family business succession scenarios—provides a tremendous amount of detail concerning these three components. Further, those details remain flexible, as people and the needs of the business itself tend to change over time. For my own succession plan at Waldron Private Wealth, I continue to refine and advance it regularly, as the project has no end date (or rather, it *does* have an end date, but that date coincides with another event that I don't want to think about).

PREPARE THE SHARES

In 2008, I reached that phase of every entrepreneur's career where I started focusing *on* the business as well as my role *in* the business. Coincidently, I was turning fifty that year and the company had entered into a mid-Maturation Phase. As Joe Robbie's story teaches us, one of the key killers of a business is the untimely death of the leader or founder whose balance sheet is dominated by the value of an illiquid business without successor leadership or a liquidity plan to pay the estate tax liability. If it is a leveraged business, the other *key* stakeholder, the bank, makes this scenario even more exposed to liquidity risk. I am fortunate in that my business model does not require debt for capital-intensive assets—we have human capital—but this did not make preparing the shares any less essential.

The first thing I wanted to do was centralize the ownership of the company in a trust for the benefit of myself, Maureen, and our heirs. Next, I wanted to provide a special business trustee to assist Maureen and our three young sons with the stewardship and decision-making of the private business. Then, I wanted to transition the current value and growth of the business outside of my taxable estate to reduce the risk of the 40 percent estate tax system. (Yes, Uncle Sam is, or *was at the time*, my 40 percent partner.) Finally, I intended to set up the platform for ownership transition of our entire family balance sheet for generations to come on a tax-efficient basis with creditor protection provisions.

A QUICK NOTE BEFORE we move on: The term "family balance sheet" is important. Unless you plan on consuming all your assets or giving them all to charity, then you are a steward, or fiduciary, for these assets for future generations. Recall the story of the client who failed to educate her son about the ethical and moral standards of stewardship and fiduciary responsibility. Senior generations have a huge opportunity to provide the platform to position and protect wealth from creditors and transfer taxes for generations to come. Do not procrastinate here either! Our process of Lifestyle vs. Legacy Assets (which we will discuss in chapter 10) helps clients frame their technical and emotional approach to managing, structuring, and investing the entire family balance sheet for multiple generations.

With all these goals in mind, I made the decision to transfer or sell all of the stock in Waldron Private Wealth, along with all other investment assets, stocks, bonds, and investment real estate to a trust for the benefit of Maureen, me, and our heirs.

PREPARE THE BUSINESS

From the time I established Waldron Private Wealth until 2011, I ran the business with my key leadership team in an informal management style. And then I decided that I needed to broaden and formalize the management of the company, so I established the executive team, gave key executives decision-making authority on strategic issues, overhauled the organizational chart, and began to invest heavily in management and leadership skills training. Before our first meeting as the new management team, we all read Michael Roberto's book *The Art of Critical*

Decision Making.[21] This book was a valuable educational tool and helped lay the groundwork for us to better understand group dynamics and how successful teams debate and make critical decisions.

In 2014, I named Matt Helfrich president, Mike Krol CFO, Ben Greenfeld CIO, and myself CEO. The four of us then spent the next four years working together to form an operating agreement that would establish the actions we would take in response to certain contingencies. I can't stress enough how important an operating agreement is to any company, as it sets the foundation for leadership transition, both now and in the future. Any good operating agreement illustrates how to determine the company's value, establishes governance, outlines the distribution policy, and identifies what happens if someone gets divorced, becomes disabled, or simply decides to leave the company.

Depending on where you are in the Entrepreneurial Lifecycle, an operating agreement might not sound like it applies to you, but keep in mind that someday your company will take on new people, and some of those people will eventually be in line to lead it in the future. By creating an operating agreement, you're essentially creating an estate plan for your company. You're thinking about all the things that could go right and all that could go wrong, and then you're illustrating exactly how to solve any problems that might arise. This can be a challenging task, and it is often time-consuming, which is part of the reason why so many leaders either procrastinate about creating an operating agreement or wind up screwing it up entirely.

What's the best way to ensure an effective operating agreement? Have honest, open conversations with everyone about what could possibly go wrong. Talk your way through scenarios related to a messy divorce. Ask the tough questions, and share your honest opinions on the best ways to get through them.

---

21 Michael A. Roberto, *The Art of Critical Decision Making* (Chantilly, VA: The Teaching Company, 2009).

Until December 31, 2017, I owned 100 percent of the company equity. But thanks to our thorough effort in creating a strong operating agreement, I was able to sell a minority interest to the executive team on that date. It felt like a Neil Armstrong moment. What seemed like "one small step" for me proved to be "one giant leap" for Waldron Private Wealth. This initial transaction, while necessary for the growth and evolution of our company, was one of the most emotionally challenging times of WPW's existence—especially for me. The good news is that, after having gone through this process, our team emerged better, faster, stronger, more aligned, and more committed to each other than ever before. As a leader and executive, I grew by leaps and bounds during this transaction.

Ultimately, I will sell more of this stock over time to make room for growth and new emerging leaders. So a core piece of my succession plan includes the operating agreement and the management structure criteria for sale of additional minority shares of the family holding.

PREPARE THE HEIRS

And speaking of family, it is every bit as important to consider their needs alongside the needs of your company's future leadership. It helps to begin by developing a family mission statement. This is a higher purpose than simply a statement about the business. Here is where the idea of family legacy (which I will discuss in more detail in the final chapter) starts to incubate. Here, you should define the roles, rights, and responsibilities of *management* vs. *ownership* to all family members and stakeholders in the plan. These are two very different positions.

Management is responsible for executing the strategic plan as defined by the CEO and ratified by the board (if one exists) or the operating agreement. For employment, an heir is entitled to fair market compensation and benefits for the position he or she holds.

Ownership, on the other hand, is the right to vote the stock and receive the dividend of excess earnings.

Whatever your mix of family and other stakeholders who will run your business in the next generation, it is most important that you communicate the plan openly and honestly with the full management team. It takes years for the next generation to figure out their skill sets, likes, and dislikes, and to mature in business. For this reason, it is necessary to educate everyone and refine the message over time. Transparency of communication will ensure that the next generation of your leadership doesn't see their future position as a birthright. Your son might have that management position in his future because he is your son, but leadership is an intangible quality based on *respect of team and peers*. Leadership respect is earned over many years.

To ensure the smoothest transition possible, preparing your heirs begins by identifying who the likely stakeholders are. The obvious ones include yourself, your spouse, your partners, your children and grandchildren, their spouses, and management. But you'll also remember how the stakeholder list from the start of this chapter included some less obvious potential stakeholders, including ex-spouses, stepchildren, your partner(s) spouse(s) and heirs, the bank, your trustee, your partner(s) trustee(s), and the board.

When you review the list of potential stakeholders, you can see how complex and potentially ugly things can get. But it only gets truly ugly if you don't communicate. In our experience, most of the succession plans that fail do so because the leader wasn't transparent in their communication. Yes, it is difficult to openly discuss the many emotional components of succession. There is so much that is unknown and so many unintended consequences to fear. But make no mistake, while succession planning is challenging, undoing a succession plan that failed (or handling the fallout if one never existed) is *really* challenging.

The importance of communication and education is why we have put so much time, energy, and resources into developing our Next

Generation Wealth Planning and Education services at Waldron Private Wealth. Through this process, we help our clients establish and share the information that the next generation will need to lead the business and manage the wealth effectively. This allows them to fully understand the *why* of the family and the business while establishing their role in both. Knowing their role will better prepare them for the challenges that will eventually be theirs, which in turn prepares them to take ownership of and responsibility for the outcomes. All of this will greatly improve the chances that your family will operate harmoniously and your business will enjoy continued success well into the future.

The Next Generation's Dilemma

One of the most difficult things for a future generation is having to make the decision to sell the business. Selling the business that has been handed down to them from the generation(s) before, a business that has been an integral part of the fiber of the family, can be heart-wrenching. Every time I've seen this, the walls of the business are covered with pictures of the founder, a history of the company, and so on. The leader from a subsequent generation sometimes has to look at those walls and make the decision to sell the business.

Such a move can feel like a betrayal of the family legacy and betrayal of past, present, and future family members. Unfortunately, given competitive industry and market dynamics, it is often the right decision, and is often time sensitive. Therefore, the luxury of working through these emotions and becoming okay with them over time just isn't there. You have to know when it's time to get out. This is where the Velocity of Decision-Making is absolutely critical. Unfortunately, we have seen situations where it dissipates a substantial portion of the multigenerational wealth created over time because that person doesn't want to be "that guy" who sold the family business. Personally, though, I would much rather be the guy who sells the family business than the guy who blew the family wealth because I held on too long.

So as a final point, never stop assessing. I hold my annual review with my planning team and special business trustee(s), estate attorney, and immediate family every December to evaluate what needs to be changed. The business will evolve, stakeholders will expand and mature, interests will change, and industries can be disrupted. All of this requires reassessing what a successful succession plan looks like on a regular basis.

Emotional Lessons:

- Keep your head on a swivel as to currents, tides, and winds in your industry. Have the self-awareness to understand if you are being dominated by your neocortex (the logic processor of your brain) or your amygdala (your emotional epicenter).
- Don't let your conflicting emotions delay you from addressing this important planning step.
- Doing nothing is a decision to avoid addressing tough issues.

Technical Strategies:

- Succession management must coexist with succession ownership. Develop and nurture your management team.
- Consider the Six Secrets to Successful Succession (say that three times fast!). No two succession plans are alike. Fortunately, most of the successful ones share six key components:

    1. They define what "success" means. It sounds trivial, but success is uniquely defined for each business and family of owners.

2. Succession leadership must understand how it coexists with the succession ownership plan.

3. They prepare the shares for transition.

4. They make sure that all stakeholders in this complex equation understand the role, rights, responsibilities, and expectations of ownership vs. leadership.

5. Everyone must understand that succession is part of the company culture. This ensures sustainability, stability, and leadership for the entire organization in the face of unforeseen events.

6. They must integrate, communicate, and educate all stakeholders about all five previous points early and often. Wash, rinse, repeat!

The Journey Is Worth It

Succession planning is difficult when you're starting it, but always keep in mind that the journey is worth it. You're building the foundation for your company's future and for future generations of your family. Your effort ensures that the second generation isn't only inheriting money and control of the company; they're also inheriting a structure, a philosophy, and a plan that they have helped to establish. They then become stewards of the plan. This positions them for better chances at success. Further, they can continue to tweak and update this plan over the years, which will help the company continue to succeed.

If you have done the succession legwork and have identified emerging talent in the firm, mentored them, and prepared them for leadership roles as an ongoing part of the firm's future, the company will be much better positioned to successfully transition after a founder or CEO steps down or passes on.

CHAPTER EIGHT

It's Decision Time!

Stakeholders:

- ✓ You
- ✓ Your spouse
- ✓ Your children and their spouses
- ✓ Your grandchildren and maybe their spouses
- ✓ Your partner(s)
- ✓ Your investors or bankers
- ✓ The management team
- ✓ Your employees
- ✓ Board members
- ✓ Ex-spouse(s)
- ✓ Stepchildren
- ✓ Partner(s) spouses
- ✓ Partner(s) heirs
- ✓ Trustee(s)
- ✓ Partner(s) trustee(s)
- ✓ Any and every stakeholder's attorney(s)

Emotions:

- ● The entire negative basket of fear, anxiety, and greed!
- ● Trust or distrust about whether you can count on your buyer or successor to do right by your employees
- ● Guilt over selling the business and depriving future generations while also disappointing past generations
- ● Responsibility related to whether you're doing well by your stakeholders and customers
- ● The list of emotions above is only partially complete. When you enter the decision-making process about how to execute the transition or sale of your businesses, you're going to be dealing with the biggest range of emotions you've ever had to manage. Yes, you've engaged with all these emotions at different points in the process, but you've never had to deal with them at this intensity level all at once. They've never been triggered by these specific reasons and with so many stakeholders' interests in play.

Symptoms:

- ● You have reached maturity and are a top performer in your industry.
- ● You are starting to contemplate pursuing other interests or passions in life.

ON THREE SEPARATE OCCASIONS over the course of nearly twenty years, our client Dan, who founded the equipment rental business, ran into the frustration that can come with deciding whether and how to transition. The first time he tried to sell his business, he fell victim to a common emotional trap: guilt. The second time, it was a combination of distrust and anger toward the potential acquirer—all negative emotions. The third time around, the stars aligned and he was able to sell.

On Dan's first attempt, family guilt slowed his Velocity of

Decision-Making. He thought he was emotionally and psychologically ready to sell to an outside buyer, but at the end of the day, he made the choice to hold onto the company so he could groom his daughter to take over. After traveling a long distance on this path and doing all the hard work of planning and preparing for a sale, he pivoted in the opposite direction. He transitioned into an aggressive growth mode, took on debt, added assets and locations, entered new growth markets, and took the business to new heights. Along the way, he did what he could to prepare his chosen successor for leadership, but eight years later, it finally became clear that his daughter did not have the same passion to run a company of this size and scope that he did.

This left Dan with a new choice to make when it came time for his second attempt at transitioning the business. Once again, he thought he was emotionally and psychologically ready to sell. This time, however, the problem was the buyer. After much research and planning, it became clear that the best strategy would be to allow the largest competitor in the industry to acquire the business. But to Dan, this felt like making a deal with the devil. The competitive bad blood between these two companies clouded the clear truth that this deal made the best sense from a price and value standpoint—for himself, for his team, and for all his stakeholders. And so, for a second time, Dan traveled a long way down the sales path before, late in the process, his distrust caused the whole transaction to fall apart. Ultimately, he couldn't see himself packaging up a company he had built with so much of his own blood, sweat, and tears and handing it over to the enemy.

Dan always knew that you're either growing or you're dying. So, after pulling the plug on this second opportunity, he again went aggressively into reinvesting in the business. He held the philosophy that you go big or go home, so he went all in, taking on $100 million in new debt to expand. I was impressed.

Another seven years later, a new buyer came along at exactly the right time, with the right fit and the right funding for the company. Finally, Dan was able to complete the transaction. Because of his stature in the industry, and partly because this is precisely what makes him tick, he held a minority interest in the company for quite a while after the sale. To Dan's dismay, years later, the financial buyer, who had no emotional overlay in the competitive landscape, ended up selling and merging with that same deal-with-the-devil competitor Dan had refused to sell to seven years prior. But since Dan held only a minority interest, he didn't have the control to nix the transaction. Fortunately, it wound up being a textbook, good merger with the right footprint, specialties, synergies, and capabilities—but it never would have been possible if the new leader of the company had allowed his emotions to disrupt the clearly perfect transaction.

As Dan's story illustrates, transition can have its challenges and rewards, but the level of challenge and reward depends almost entirely on your ability to control your emotions. In this chapter, we will examine the matters to consider as you approach your own transition, along with the emotions you will need to get under control in order to maximize the reward for yourself, your business's future, your family, and your stakeholders.

How Do You Know When It's Time?

As the leader of a successful business, it's time to start thinking about transition when one or more of these four specific concerns enter your mind:

1. There are stakeholders in your life who have worked hard to make your business what it is today, and you want to reward them for that effort.
2. The business is fundamentally changing, and the people currently in leadership no longer have the energy to guide it through these changes.

3. You feel like some of your stakeholders might be better equipped than you to take this business to greater heights or ensure its longevity.
4. You want to free up time to pursue other passions.

These thoughts and feelings are difficult enough to manage when family *isn't* involved. By the time most business leaders reach this point in the Entrepreneurial Lifecycle, there is almost always family to consider. This requires a lot of soul-searching. With family succession, powerful emotions like love, guilt, and a desire for fairness can complicate the decision. A few of the many questions you may ask yourself include, *Which heir for which position? When is the right time to have the conversation with my family about my plan to step aside?* and *When and how do I talk to them about the wealth that this transfer will generate?* The answers to these questions are never simple, because the inextricable connection between money, power, and emotion comes into play.

Because the emotional component is so tangled and tricky, many entrepreneurs make the mistake of holding on to control of the business for too long. It is wonderful to be blessed with the opportunity to lead a business that either you or your family started. But doing so in times when industries are being disrupted, competition is global and sometimes unfair, and market demographics have changed tremendously ratchets up the risks associated with holding on for too long. As companies like Kodak, Sears, and Blockbuster have shown us, there's also the potential for catastrophe if your decision-making is slowed by the choppy waters of emotion and you can't make the bold, unemotional decision to radically change the business model, sell, or merge with a competitor.

Often, without fresh ideas, energized management, and emotionally unencumbered leadership, the fear is that, like Kodak, you could see everything you've worked for rendered obsolete overnight. Many have shared with me the thought that "if I sell, that means I have given up or even failed." I hold the opposite view. If you sell, then you have demonstrated the strength to fight through your ego and the courage to make a bold decision that will benefit all stakeholders.

Yes, the emotional component related to how to manage everyone's expectations regarding who will get what after the sale or succession can be unpleasant, but it's a lot better than potentially damaging the stakeholders' value by not being able to make the bold decision to stay ahead of the competition. The earlier you begin these conversations with your stakeholders and the potential future leaders of your company—whether they are the next generation of family and management leaders or new equity owners or partners—the smoother the transition will be. Not to mention the positive impact this will have on the enterprise value. The education process is a long one, but your probability of successfully transitioning your business to an appealing buyer or the next generation of leadership correlates directly with how early you start the conversation and how thorough your planning becomes.

If none of the above motivates you—if you're not transitioning for the benefit of your family or for your own emotional sanity—then consider greed as a positive motivator. For every business, there comes a point during the Maturation Phase when you harness your traction, turn it into momentum, and then accelerate to maturity. "Maturity" is defined as operational expertise and efficiency that puts you in the top quartile (or higher) of performers in your industry. Achieving this state means that you have developed a management team and honed your executive skills in presiding over the team. It also means that your business's value is higher than ever.

Preparation for transition can have an incredibly positive impact on enterprise value. Think about it this way: The succession process requires management training, and therefore, maturation for the business. Whether you're currently a seller or not, the market will always put a premium on the quality of the management team. Good management operates more efficiently, which is reflected in the margins, a higher Velocity of Decision-Making, and ultimately, higher earnings before interests, taxes, depreciation, and amortization (EBITDA). In this situation, Gordon Gekko is correct: "Greed is good." So if it's not clear from an emotional standpoint that the time is right to sell, then maybe the answer will become clearer if you think of the matter in purely financial terms.

The Four Paths

During the Maturation Phase, every entrepreneur will come to a split in the road that leads off in four different directions. Depending on the dynamics of the industry, you could run into this decision several times. The four paths are:

1. The Lifestyle Path: Accept it, live a comfortable life, and quit caring about lost opportunity. Some do follow this route, and who's to say they're wrong?
2. The Double-Down Path: Reinvest, re-leverage, hire, expand, and seize the opportunity that your wisdom and hard work have created. Dan's approach!
3. The Chips-Off-the-Table Path: Bring on a carefully vetted strategic partner who will allow you to reduce your risk in the business and put a little money in your pocket. This is something of a middle ground between the Double-Down Path and the Get-Out Path.
4. The Get-Out Path: Sell the business or transition it to the next generation of leadership.

There is no right or wrong answer here. The unique and beautiful thing about entrepreneurship in America is that *you* built it, so you can do whatever you want with it, whenever you want. In my experience, most choose the Double-Down Path more than once. Depending on age, energy, and assessment of company capabilities, the Maturation Phase typically concludes with the Chips-Off-the-Table Path or the Get-Out Path, so you better prepare for it.

THE LIFESTYLE PATH

The typical symptoms of a business that is about to take (or has already taken) the Lifestyle Path include:

- Debt has been paid off (or at least it has reached a comfortable level)
- An adequate number of stable customers
- A predictable, comfortable, and stable annual income from the business
- A respectable personal balance sheet
- Owner(s) who are reluctant to reinvest in the business or risk the business or personal balance sheet
- Owner(s) who don't want to overcomplicate the business with management layers, geographic locations, or product lines

This condition can be fine for the current owner(s) of the business, as long as they're aware it's happening. At Waldron Private Wealth, our job is to drive the discussion so that clients on the Lifestyle Path understand where they are and how it impacts them, the company, their personal wealth management decisions, and all stakeholders involved. Depending on the severity of the condition, the business itself is likely losing operating efficiency, market share, employee morale and energy, stature in the industry, talent (due to all of the above), and opportunity (of all sorts, including new customers, new talent, income, and enterprise value, to name a few). Often, we have to point out that not making a business decision is a decision not to act. This is the most clear signal that a business on the Lifestyle Path has suffered the divergence of the two *whys*.

THE DOUBLE-DOWN PATH

As Dan's story illustrates, the catalyst for this decision is a moment that requires you to make a bold new decision. You know you're facing a point in your company's history that will require you to take on more time, risk, and leadership. At this point, you find yourself asking, *Am I really up for this kind of challenge again?* Sometimes you also wonder, *Am I still the best person to lead this business to the next level?* This is a moment of honest self-reflection.

Many of our clients choose to double-down after a "risk time-out." I have personally experienced this several times. It is like climbing the mountain and reaching a plateau or goal, and then taking a pause before you scale the next ridge. If you pitch a tent in this spot, then you're taking a pause. If you build a house there, then you have chosen the Lifestyle Path.

THE CHIPS-OFF-THE-TABLE PATH

Here we find the (often comfortable) middle ground between doubling down and selling or transitioning completely out of the business. There might come a time during your Lifecycle when you start thinking about vetting a partner to bring on board. If this person is an equity partner, then it allows you to take some of your money and risk off the table. Where before, you owned 100 percent of the business, maybe now you can own 80 percent, 60 percent, 51 percent, or less than 50 percent (if you don't mind giving up operational control). Either way, this path usually means that you will have less equity, less ownership (which means that your vote will weigh less), and potentially less operational control. On the other hand, it also allows you to step away from the business more often and have more free time for yourself, your family, and your other pursuits in life.

The main lesson here is that you must be sure to vet this partner (or partners) carefully. Next, define the operating agreement in a way that aligns your skill set with that of your new partner. The operating agreement must be thorough enough to outline what happens in the event of death, divorce, or disability, how power transfers when one or more partners decides to leave the company, and what everyone's role is prior to and after any such transition.

THE GET-OUT PATH

Everyone will eventually have to prepare for sale or transition, as it will happen at some point, one way or another. When you approach this path, the matter becomes even more complicated, as now you face another fork in the road with two *more* paths you can take:

1. Transition to family leadership or ownership
2. Sell all or part of the business to a third party

You know you have reached this new fork in the road when circumstances have changed. The *feeling* has changed. You are no longer like the Wright Brothers wondering if this business will fly; now you're more like a fighter pilot wondering if you still have the energy and desire to control your business's momentum while maneuvering in and out of storms, dodging missiles, and taking down the competition. This can be challenging—and exhilarating.

Get-Out Path #1: Transition

Family businesses follow this path frequently. In these situations, the leader decides it's time to step back. They get away from the day-to-day and appoint their heirs to leadership positions—CEO, president, CFO, CIO, and so on. Then they begin transitioning into a more advisory role like becoming a board member. This allows them to continue providing input while remaining free to pursue other interests. Again, hopefully you have been working on your succession plan and operating agreement, because this path means that it's time to execute.

Get-Out Path #2: Sell to a Third Party

If you decide to sell the business, then this path can take on any number of forms. You could sell to a private equity partner, to a competitor, to the management team, or a combination of these. You could sell a portion of your interest or sell the business completely. Whatever the case, selling implies, "Give me a check. Here's the business. I'm out." For many business owners—particularly when there is less of the family component involved—this is the cleanest, simplest path to take.

In our experience, the majority of the time, when you sell your business outright, it is best for you, as the founding entrepreneur, to arrange for a short-lived relationship with the business post-transaction. In other words, it is better to stay on with a shorter-term employment agreement (say, six months or so) rather than the kind of longer-term agreement that sometimes applies to a family business situation. This is particularly true if you sell either to private equity or a company that has a lot of management bureaucracy. Usually, these kinds of buyers will have a different agenda and organizational culture, and your input in such a situation can become counterproductive—or worse yet, it can be ignored.

Another variation of this path is divestiture. Divestiture implies that there are steps you and your buyer must take before the transition is complete. And "complete" is defined as 100 percent ownership transition, a substantial minority, or anywhere in between. As I have mentioned, I am engaged in this process right now at our company, delegating certain leadership responsibilities to key stakeholders in my management team. This has been a valuable strategy, as not only does it help prepare for a smoother leadership transition should I decide to step down, but in the meantime, it also expands the way the company is managed. This has further allowed me to blend family and nonfamily members into the future leadership structure of the company. Think of divestiture as something of a hybrid between transitioning ownership and selling. You don't sell or retire or give up all your control; you phase in new leadership and ownership over time.

Divestiture also allows you to retain some measure of control over your company's direction while also bringing in ideas from new (and often younger) leaders who see the industry in a different perspective. A client of mine has done this several times during his company's Maturation Phase, and now, given his age and the status and structure of the business, he recognizes that he is done as the full-time leader of the business. He doesn't have family to pass it on to, he knows he will be fine financially if he transitions out, but he still wants to remain engaged with the business and involved in the industry. For his situation, divestiture makes perfect sense.

The path you choose is entirely dependent on where you are in life and in the business, who your stakeholders are, and how you want your life to look after the business is no longer completely under your control.

Don't Let Guilt Slow Your Velocity of Decision-Making

There are times when leaders become so concerned with family and legacy matters that they put off making the valuable leadership transition decisions until it's too late. If you are the founder of your business, there is a chance that at some point you will start to think of it not just as your *hope*, but as your *obligation* to pass this business on to the next generation. Sometimes, this can cause the leader to hold on for too long. They will wait for that perfect inflection point when the business is as healthy and profitable as possible and when the heirs are completely prepared to lead. Reread that last sentence and tell me what is wrong with this picture. If you wait for a clear signal that now is the ideal time to sell, it will never happen, and you will miss your opportunity.

Alternately, we have seen many instances when second-, third-, and fourth-generation businesses are too slow in their decision-making because they feel like they're dishonoring the wishes of prior generations to keep the business within the family and maintain the family legacy. Sometimes, they also feel like they could be depriving future generations of the opportunities they received. (Ah, the powerful self-inflicted guilt trip.) They feel like it's their obligation to transition only to family members, even if the writing is on the wall that a new direction would benefit the company. Sometimes changes in industries require decisive, bold, timely decisions that can be tough, especially with the ghosts of the past and the hopes of future generations swirling in your mind.

With that emotional backdrop of self-inflicted guilt, keep in mind that a slow Velocity of Decision-Making can cause significant deterioration not only in the health of the business (and your health), but also in your wealth. Wanting to find the perfect strategy for both the past and future generations can inflict serious harm on an otherwise healthy and successful company. At Waldron Private Wealth, we have seen this many times, so we try to emphasize to our clients that families can take big hits to their balance sheets simply because they aren't able to respond quickly and decisively when the situation calls for it. Again, family wealth management and business ownership issues are inextricably connected.

Emotional Lessons:

- If you elect to keep the status quo, consult your inner voice and make sure you realize that "no decision is a conscious decision."
- If you elect to transition the business to the next generation, the first step is figuring out how to take your hands off the wheel and relinquish your current position and control in a way that will keep the business running without causing too much emotional strife.
- For the greatest chance of success in transitioning, integrate, communicate, and educate your management and heirs about your vision and their roles.

- Understand that transitions can sometimes break down. The difference between successful transitions and not-so-successful ones is preparation and communication. If you approach your transition with a "set it and forget it" mentality, then it will inevitably face challenges along the way. So, as the owner of the business, you need to remain involved with the transition, no matter how emotionally ready you may be to step back and let someone else take the wheel.

- Keep in mind that a successful transition may come at the cost of up-front consideration. An outright sale gives you the ability to maximize the price you receive for the business. That is rarely the case with family leadership transitions.

Technical Strategies:

- Integrate, communicate, and educate the next generation of leadership and heirs as soon as possible.
- Choose your path (Lifestyle, Double-Down, Chips Off the Table, or Get Out), get familiar with it, and consult all stakeholders with honest self-reflection.
- Coordinate the family wealth issues with the business issues.
- Construct the right team to help you execute your decision. You will know you have the right team when you are in conflict or possibly angry with them. This means that they are willing to tell you what you don't want to hear, which is always valuable advice.
- The business is probably the largest concentrated stock on your family balance sheet. As such, it represents the biggest reward, but also the biggest risk. So, before you make your decision, think about the entire family balance sheet, not just the business. We have counseled many clients who have had trouble with this, even in cases where the family balance sheet has grown to eclipse the business value.

So Much Anxiety

Your emotional investment in the company is only one of the many considerable anxieties that threaten to get in your way as you ponder whether it is time for you to transition out of or sell the company. Doubt and second-guessing also cause anxiety. Most entrepreneurs have never sold a company before, so they don't fully understand the process. Many questions need answers: What will happen to your employees? What becomes of the legacy of the business and the reputation and brand after the sale? Will your employees be disappointed? What about your customers? Will your vendors see their synergies with the company change? Naturally, all these relationships and unanswered questions create a ton of anxiety and uncertainty. And those are only the *start* of what I call the soft anxieties.

Those soft anxieties continue as the questions turn inward, toward the matters of time and personal fulfillment: *What will I do with all this extra time? What do I want to pursue? How will I feel as fulfilled in my day-to-day life when I don't have a company to run anymore?* Often, for the first time in years (if not decades), the business leader will start wondering what his or her interests are and worrying about how he or she will stay engaged. There is a huge social component as well. Much of one's personal and social networking is wrapped up in their role as president, CEO, or founder of their company. We hear questions like, "When I'm no longer running the business, will I be viewed differently?" "What will I do when I wake up in the morning after the transition?" and "I can't really play golf five days a week, can I?" We also hear from the spouse, "She is retiring, not me. I have my daily routine! How will she change that?" Ideally, the leader has been thinking about the answers to these questions for a long time already, but you would be surprised how many haven't!

Next are what I call the hard anxieties: "How much money am I going to get out of this deal after tax?" "Will it be enough to support my lifestyle and my family's lifestyle?" "What exactly does my lifestyle cost, anyway?" "What do I do with the assets that the buyer doesn't want?" Most business owners don't know the answers to these questions because the lines between their personal and professional lives are decidedly blurred. Getting the answers to these questions typically requires a substantial amount of forensic accounting, because much of the personal lifestyle ends up being born and buried within the financials of the business.

For all these reasons and all these complexities, in the next chapter, we will explore the rigors of the sale process so you can avoid being blindsided by the soft anxieties, hard anxieties, and all the other pitfalls associated with this challenging period in the Lifecycle.

Preparing the Business for the Sale

Stakeholders:

- ✓ You
- ✓ Your spouse
- ✓ Your children and their spouses
- ✓ Your grandchildren and maybe their spouses
- ✓ Your partner(s)
- ✓ Your investors or bankers
- ✓ The management team
- ✓ Your employees
- ✓ Board members
- ✓ Ex-spouse(s)
- ✓ Stepchildren
- ✓ Partner(s) spouses
- ✓ Partner(s) heirs
- ✓ Trustee(s)
- ✓ Partner(s) trustee(s)
- ✓ Any and every stakeholder's attorney(s)

Emotions:

- ● Fear and excitement about what comes next
- ● Anxiety over everything involved in the transaction and what your life will be like after the transaction
- ● Confidence and doubt that you are ready to sell or transition out of your business
- ● Gratification about the journey you have been on
- ● Sadness about losing the baby you have nurtured all your life
- ● Greed as you pursue the highest price
- ● Fatigue from the daily fight over what that price (and dozens of other terms) will be
- ● Guilt about those you've deprived of the opportunity to lead the business even further
- ● Guilt about the stakeholders you will leave behind when you exit

Symptoms:

- ● You are wanting to pursue other life interests, and now you're asking yourself questions like:
  - ⊘ "Do I have the stamina to do this again?"
  - ⊘ "Do I have the desire?"
  - ⊘ "Do I have the right team in place to take over successfully?"
  - ⊘ "Has the business environment changed to where a new set of eyes (or perhaps skills) might benefit the company's future?"
  - ⊘ "Are there other passions in life that I might prefer to pursue?"

WHEN A BUSINESS LEADER reaches the point in the process where it's time to get out, they often tell us, "I have lost my passion for the business" or even, "I've never actually pursued my true passion because I was always so busy running this business." Sometimes that sense of obligation was to their stakeholders. Other times, they felt predestined to run the family business. In these cases, the leader never had passion; they had a job.

If you find this particular brand of self-awareness taking over, you face a difficult decision. You will feel an intense sense of betrayal of the stakeholders. The epiphany that counters this—the one that allows the business leader to make this tough decision in the first place—is the realization that you have been betraying *yourself* all along. Selling or transitioning your business is all about life, liberty, and the pursuit of happiness. When this epiphany occurs, the decision becomes easy, and the guilt, while it never completely leaves, gets more manageable.

Sometimes, you can prepare for arriving at this crossroads. Other times, you don't see it coming until you're standing right on it. In this respect, one client of ours is particularly amazing. Even in his midsixties, he still had his hand on the throttle, aggressively pushing forward. At a board meeting, the conversation centered on looking for acquisitions to expand footprint and capacity.

Then, one day, without warning, the plan was disrupted. The company got pulled into a political and public lawsuit—one of those situations where everyone in the zip code of the event got named. The conflict played out in the media and tarnished (and without substantiation) the reputation of a great company and a proud man. Through this legal process, he wound up being dominated by the co-defendant in the lawsuit, an 800-pound gorilla who also happened to be his largest customer. This left him feeling humiliated, furious, insecure, and helpless to control his own destiny. All he could do was sit and wait for the next article to come out—which were all riddled with half-truths—and for what wound up being *years* of litigation.

There came a point when I saw the winds simply go dead in his sails. "I like playing offense, not defense," he said at a board meeting. And with that, the conversation changed from acquisition to sale.

Sometimes, the decision that it is time to get out can be self-evident, like when the circumstances become impossible to ignore. Those circumstances can be either positive or negative (either way, hopefully they don't involve litigation and the press). The positive: You're in a hot growth industry that makes sale or succession particularly attractive right now; you have a unique, motivated buyer; your chosen successor has proven him or herself to be ready to take this business to the next level. The negative: death, disability, disruption, and debt. As this story illustrates, there is no way to predict or sugarcoat the negative side—those four Ds can be devastating to any plan, particularly when it involves sale or succession.

The Hard Financials and Soft Psychologicals of Selling a Business

In today's environment of low interest rates, strong economic activity, and abundance of capital and risk appetites, it's a seller's market. Strategic buyers want to acquire businesses so they can capture the opportunity in an economic environment that rewards consolidation and inorganic growth. Venture capital and private equity is flush with cash to pursue opportunities, which, given the current conditions, bids up price. Some business owners who wouldn't otherwise be sellers wind up entertaining offers at multiples unlike anything they've seen before, and it starts to look like a nice time to sell.

Currently, Waldron Private Wealth is working with clients who are both buyers and sellers from all industries. We are helping companies with hypergrowth in hot industries, second-generation leaders in manufacturing who want to sell due to a change in market dynamics and competitive conditions, and leaders who would *not* otherwise be sellers if not for those proposed multiples. In our experience, there are right ways and wrong ways to approach every transition.

As I have said before, no two journeys in entrepreneurship are identical. Sometimes, you know that you want out and you know how to get out. Other times, someone will make an offer you can't refuse (which obviously makes the decision easy). Still other times, you've been operating under the expectation that this is a family business that will be passed down. Then, like Dan (see chapter 8), you realize that your heirs don't actually *want* to run the business. In these cases, selling the business is the only exit.

In my experience, the most successful transitions—whether by sale or succession to the next generation of management—are those that were prepared years, and not months, in advance. Obviously, though, circumstances sometimes dictate the timeline, and lengthy preparation isn't possible. Conversely, with the luxury of time, the probability of success is increased, but not guaranteed. What matters most is that you understand the "hard" financial implications on your life and on the lives of your stakeholders, you have familiarized yourself with the highly complicated *sale process*, and you have prepared for the "soft" psychological issues.

This is a highly emotional process that requires extreme self-control and focus on the transaction objectives. Your conviction will be tested often. It's all a matter of understanding the process and the hard financial issues while not being emotionally hijacked by the ever-present soft psychological issues. The best advice for tackling both is to commit to rigorous pre-transaction and post-transaction planning.

The Importance of Pre-Transaction and Post-Transaction Planning

Most owners have never been through the sale process before. If you choose to sell, there are now two major preparations to make:

1. Prepare the business for the sale
2. Prepare the owner(s) for the sale

These are two very different preparations. Because of this, at Waldron Private Wealth, we have developed a pre-transaction and post-transaction process where we help prepare entrepreneurs and their business (on both the hard financial and soft psychological issues) for a successful transaction. We engage with questions like: How do you make the company most financially attractive? Are there any management changes you need to make? How do you make this transaction the most income tax efficient? How do you position the shares in the plan for optimal estate tax planning? Where will your income come from post-sale? What does your lifestyle demand? Where do charity and your philanthropic desires fit into this? How do you surgically separate your personal and business life, both financially and psychologically? All of these must be considered.

Once we have answered these questions, we can move on to the two major preparations: preparing the business and preparing the owners. In this chapter, we will discuss the former. For more information on the latter, please see chapter 10.

Preparing the business deals with the hard financial and organizational considerations. The process will be more impactful the earlier it starts. As a bonus, most of the steps in the process are good business practices that help lead to a more efficiently run company.

For as long as you've been running this business, you have probably thought about it like this: *I own a business*. But if you break it down, what you have owned all these years is more like a stock—or more directly, like the largest concentrated stock on your family balance sheet. Over the years, it has provided you with a healthy return. Now that the time has come to sell it, you're looking at the biggest reward yet, but also the highest level of risk. To maximize that return and minimize that risk, you're going to have to undergo quite a bit of due diligence.

Think about all the hard work that people go through to sell their houses—deciding whether to use a broker, choosing a broker, running market comparisons, decluttering, repainting, staging, and so on. We perform all of this difficult labor when trying to sell our house, but we don't think about it when it comes time to sell our business. This is particularly strange, since selling a business is *much* harder than selling a house, the return is substantially higher, and the risk of losing some of that return is also substantially higher.

The steps to maximize return and minimize risk include a deep dive into the following:

GET LEAN

If you cut the fat and increase efficiency to drive earnings before interest, tax, depreciation, and amortization (EBITDA), then you increase your company's valuation. Looking in every corner of the organization for expense savings can help boost cash flow and earnings. Instilling this discipline early can generate more current cash flow, year in and year out. It also increases the buyer's confidence that management can operate efficiently, which in turn also increases value.

UNDERSTAND AND SEARCH FOR ALL ADD BACKS

Add backs are those expenses that do not directly impact the core business. In private businesses, many of the expenses support the owner's *personal* lifestyle. Focus on the costs and benefits—the people who provide them and the people who receive them. This analysis is difficult because the owner (seller) and the business have grown inextricably together, often since inception. It is essential, however, because the cost that your company incurs to support your family and your lifestyle is added back to earnings, and therefore increases EBITDA to which the multiple is applied. In other words, if you do this detailed analysis in advance and are prepared to defend these add backs, then you get a *higher price* for the business.

DEVELOP THE MANAGEMENT TEAM AND UPDATE THE ORGANIZATION CHART

This step involves hiring, firing, training, and reshuffling. Buyers see a lot of value in a well-constructed organization chart and a deep management team capable of executing a strategic plan. Update your organization chart to reflect the skills of the team and the direction the company is going. Once the chart is complete, you can train management to lead and execute accordingly.

TIGHTEN DOWN FINANCIAL REPORTING AND CONTROLS

The more comfortable the buyer is with the quality of the financial reporting, the smoother the due diligence will go. Being prepared for what the buyers will want to see will expedite the process as well. While it isn't always required, being able to share audited statements extending back two years prior is usually a worthwhile investment. As an alternative, you could consider having a quality of earnings report conducted by an independent CPA firm.

DEVELOP A VISION AND A STRATEGIC PLAN TO ACCOMPLISH THAT VISION

During the sale process, your team will likely be arguing for a higher price based not only on current EBITDA but also on future opportunity. If you have a clear vision of that opportunity and a detailed strategic plan for management to execute, that makes it easier for your team to sell the *sizzle* in addition to the *steak*. This includes positioning the business for opportunistic growth in the right markets and with the right products or services.

TIE UP THE NEGATIVE LOOSE ENDS

Negative loose ends can include legal or regulatory issues, struggling divisions or markets, capitalization table matters, shareholder disputes, corporate structure, and tax or compliance issues. Whatever you can do to eliminate existing contingent liabilities will go a long way toward simplifying the due diligence process. This is especially important because a long due diligence process can increase the probability of what we call "deal fatigue."

CLEANUP OPERATIONS AND THE BALANCE SHEET

This cleanup involves terminating underperforming markets, divisions, or departments—anything that could be accretive to earnings. Also, scrub the balance sheet for non-core business assets. Get rid of them and the expense associated with them. During this process, you might find hidden issues or asset value.

Hidden asset value can wreak havoc on a sale. For instance, consider real estate value. In many cases, buyers don't want to purchase the real estate (among many other company assets) from the seller. There are a multitude of reasons for this, including unknown environmental liability. The most common reason is that not purchasing the real estate gives the buyer flexibility to relocate the business or its divisions, folding them into the buyer's other operations or friendlier regulatory or tax jurisdictions. When buyers don't buy the real estate, the seller and his or her family can by default find themselves having to manage a real estate holding company after the sale.

A client of ours runs a manufacturing business with some extremely valuable real estate on which some of the operations are located. The business is facing competitive challenges from China, the European Union (EU), and other government-subsidized jurisdictions. In addition, it is a mature industry with a high cost of capital, shrinking operating margins, and customer purchasing power. The management team is currently focused on an operational turnaround, but in reality, the highest opportunity for family return on assets is to manage the real estate opportunity and dispose of the operating business. It's the McDonald's Effect, where real estate value is greater than enterprise value.

BUILD AN ALL-STAR TRANSACTION TEAM

As I mentioned earlier, there is nothing more expensive than bad legal advice. The same holds true with investment bankers. An investment banker serves a vital role in helping owners of private businesses sell their companies. A good investment banker will perform some or all of the following with the team:

- Educate and coach the owner on the transaction process and goal setting
- Prepare the company for sale
- Help prepare the marketing document: the confidential information memorandum (CIM)
- Control information dissemination and confidentiality during the process
- Identify potential strategic buyers
- Develop the "go to market" strategy
- Structure the transaction
- Negotiate your position with the potential buyer to keep you *out* of the negotiating room so your emotions won't get in the way

Running a process to select an investment banker who is best aligned with the unique characteristics of your business is imperative. Keep in mind that "best" is not always about the ability to achieve maximum price. You want an investment banker who truly understands your company, your culture, and your goals. Anyone who frames his or her pitch around the ability to get the highest price should raise red flags, as this kind of narrow focus is often a recipe for disaster.

Beyond the investment banker, the transaction team should also include your CPA or tax advisor, your attorney, and your personal financial advisor. This team will know the financial, legal, and tax matters better than you will, but remember, *no one* knows your business better than you do. Since you'll have so many specialized experts in the room, it's important to structure the team meetings as strategic, collaborative, and transparent. A well-functioning team well help you secure a deal with the best terms possible.

HAVE A REASONABLE TIMELINE

When people arrive at the conclusion that it is time to sell their business, the tendency is to want to have the transaction close next month. This is an unreasonable expectation. There are so many time-consuming processes between day one and the closing day to consider. You must vet and hire an investment banker; work with that banker to get bids on the business; negotiate the legally binding document that formalizes the buyer's and seller's intentions related to the agreement (a document known as the Letter of Intent [LOI]); agree to the LOI; and finally, execute the sale. Be prepared for a lengthy process. In our experience, it takes an average of six months from start to finish, and as you will see in the next section, this tends to be one of the most emotional six-month periods of the Entrepreneurial Lifecycle.

MAKE SURE THAT YOU AND YOUR BUSINESS ARE
READY FOR THE TRANSACTION

This is a key final point because the timing tends to sneak up on people. The process of preparing for the sale can take quite a bit of time and effort, but then, once you have agreed to the LOI and it is time for the actual transaction to happen, this part of the process tends to move more quickly and more intensely than ever before.

Any good investment banker will tell you that in today's market, the time between LOI and purchase agreement is compressed. What used to take ninety days instead takes forty-five days, and the timelines will continue to shrink. So, prior to committing to the process, make sure you are either staffed up or have an investment banker who can provide the proper support.

Managing the Emotions of Selling a Business

Once you have done your pre-transaction planning and have prepared the business for sale, it's time for the transaction. As with succession planning, I'm not going to perform a deep dive into how investment bankers find and vet potential buyers, handle negotiations, or structure the intricacies of the definitive agreement. These topics are better suited for your investment banker and attorney to address. As long as you have assembled your all-star transaction team, they will watch out for these matters for you.

What we *can* discuss are the emotional pitfalls to avoid. The process of selling can be one of the most emotionally volatile steps in the Entrepreneurial Lifecycle. You're negotiating on behalf of many different stakeholders and interests, which introduces a huge number of variables. So let's focus on the emotional, human challenges that you will need to confront.

INVOKE THE 24-HOUR RULE

When the transaction process begins, your buttons *will* get pushed. If your buyer raises doubt about certain elements of your business in an effort to drive the price down, you can't take it personally—even if they question *you*, your team, your leadership, your business decisions, or your stewardship. Whenever you feel yourself beginning to get angry, try to remind yourself that this is purely a *business transaction*. They're not trying to insult you; they're negotiating.

The best advice I can give is this: Don't react immediately. Invoke the 24-hour rule. Get out of the emotionally charged moment, and give it 24 hours so your cerebral cortex can take back control from the limbic center. I have seen sellers whose lack of self-control completely blew up a perfectly good transaction. Giving yourself time to cool off can be a valuable strategy for avoiding this common pitfall.

UNDERSTAND YOUR POSITION VS. THE BUYER'S POSITION

Keep in mind that, as the seller, the transaction is much more personal for you. It's about so much more than getting the highest price with the lowest tax bill. For the buyer, meanwhile, this is just a transaction. Trying to think of this as an unemotional transaction will prevent you from taking things too personally (and it *will* get personal). I have seen situations where the seller thought they could part with the business, but at the eleventh hour, they pulled the plug on the deal because they just couldn't do it. So make sure you are mentally prepared to exit.

SET GOALS

While the all-star transaction team is being assembled, we counsel our clients to set their goals for the transaction. We begin by asking the seller to define what a successful transaction looks like. Then we have them set their priorities for the optimal transaction outcome. After they finish this exercise, oftentimes clients are surprised to see that their number one goal is *not* about getting the highest price.

One client of ours is going through a sale at the time of this writing, and *price* was number eight on his list of priorities, a list that included the following:

1. Eliminate future liabilities for his family
2. Minimize reps and warranties and escrow holdback
3. No earn-outs or requirements for owner to stay on
4. Sell the entire company together, no separate divisions—all or none
5. Ensure confidentiality of the process for employees, customers,

and suppliers for as long as possible. There's no upside to sparking premature speculation.

6. Secure two-year employment contracts for key leaders
7. Commit to timely completion (i.e., run an efficient process so that deal fatigue doesn't set in)
8. Get the highest price
9. Manage the stress load of the owner during the process
10. Ensure legacy continuance (i.e., the buyer will retain the company name and culture)
11. Sell the real estate with the business

SET *REALISTIC* EXPECTATIONS

The emphasis is on the word "realistic," especially when it comes to the price, because the tendency is to set unrealistic expectations that involve huge numbers. This can lead to disappointment when you start talking about the post-tax, post-earn-out, post-holdback, and post-rolled equity. A huge part of pre-transaction planning is using your team to help set your expectations.

Long before you get to the LOI, you need to identify three different thresholds for the numbers you're hoping to bring in: the *perfect world* threshold, the *acceptable* threshold, and the *no freaking way* threshold. Having an understanding of these thresholds will give you a broader perspective of how to navigate the structuring of the sale. It will allow you to prioritize during that crucial period between LOI and the purchase agreement—that period when the diligence must be at its peak and energy is usually at its lowest. The most common error in any negotiation is a business owner saying, "Well, I'd sell it for x" without first understanding the various paths they can take to get to that number. So it's really important to get your expectations in check.

DECIDE UP FRONT HOW MUCH LONGER YOU'RE WILLING TO LEAD (OR EVEN WORK FOR) THIS COMPANY

"Seven weeks, three days, four hours, and twenty-six minutes."

That was the response I got from a client who had recently sold his business when I asked, "How's it going?" His answer referred to the time he had left on his employment obligation after selling.

This is why it is so important to manage expectations related to how much longer you're going to be leading (or even working for) this company. Many business owners make the mistake of assuming that they will remain invaluable to the company for years after the sale. You must realize that, for the buyer, your business is a means to an end. They don't have the emotional investment in it that you do. It sounds cruel, but at the end of the day, it's a business decision. So what does this mean? It means that the buyer will tell you exactly what you want to hear— anything that helps them get the asset they want and that generates the return they need. This can include fudging a little on what they will expect of you after the sale. So, keep this key piece of advice in mind: Regardless of what anyone tells you, there is a good chance you will not be in the business six months after you sell.

The issue of the owner staying on after the closing is an interesting one. Regardless of the monetary earn-out terms or the employment contract, the arrangement almost never ends well for a founding owner. This is especially true in situations involving a financial buyer and not a strategic buyer. It's really difficult as a founding owner to come to work every day and see that your opinion doesn't matter anymore (if the new leadership of your company even *asks* for it). You will have to stand by and watch people be fired, laid off, or witness other management decisions that will absolutely drive you crazy. It's tough to go from general to lieutenant. Most often, these arrangements last less than one year. The shortest we have seen is three weeks.

The process of selling a business can be one of the most exhausting experiences of your business life. The emotions are intense, and your commitment to your decision will be challenged many times along the way. If you are to have a successful outcome, then understanding the process and preparing for its challenges is imperative. Expend all the time and research necessary to build a dedicated and adept professional team that can help walk you through this gauntlet.

Yes, there is quite a bit of work ahead of you, but take heart in the benefits. Not only will you secure better terms for the sale, but performing the pre-transaction planning steps will also put you ahead of the learning curve for the job you will find yourself in as soon as the sale is complete. That job? Managing a very different balance sheet for yourself and your heirs.

Emotional Lessons:

- Get comfortable with and confident in your decision to exit—otherwise, you will second-guess yourself as you progress through this emotional process.
- Address the hard financial issues and prepare for the soft psychological issues.
- Determine your goals list for the sale.
- Learn to manage your anxiety related to the volatility of public markets. The conflict between greed and security will be challenging during this period.
- Use the 24-hour rule to control visceral emotional reactions.

Technical Strategies:

- Understand the sale process and prepare the business for sale.
- Get the business "lean and clean."
- Select an all-star transaction team to guide you. Then trust their advice.
- Perform the forensic accounting analysis to separate your personal life expenses from the business expenses to understand adjusted EBITDA. Then prepare to defend those add backs for valuation.

Do Not Underestimate the Effort

Too often we see entrepreneurs make the decision to transition and then begin to focus on the next adventure in their life. The process of selling a business can be grueling, but it is one of the most important steps in the entrepreneurial journey. When an individual makes the decision to move on from the ownership and management of the business via sale or succession, it is important to understand the physical energy and emotional challenges that lie ahead to successfully accomplish your transition goals. It is the last hill to climb, but it may feel like summiting Mount Everest. After the transition, you will have a realistic expectation of what life looks like on the other side. If done right, you will optimize the value for you and your family and put the company in a position for future success.

The Day After

CHAPTER TEN

Preparing for Life after the Business

Stakeholders:

- ✓ You
- ✓ Your spouse
- ✓ Your heirs
- ✓ Your chosen charities

Emotions:

- ✓ Separation anxiety because you have just given up the entity you have nurtured for such a long time
- ✓ Security because of that large new deposit in your account
- ✓ Anxiety about how to manage these different assets and *visible* public market volatility
- ✓ Insecurity because you are no longer in control
- ✓ Frustration with your situation, especially if you are now working with (sorry, *for*) the new owners
- ✓ Confusion about life's new meaning and what gets you out of bed in the morning (much like an outgoing president must feel

when he leaves office, "Yesterday, everyone wanted to talk to me; today, my opinion doesn't matter.")

- ● Loneliness because your opinion no longer matters

Symptoms:

- ● Your Velocity of Decision-Making has hit the brakes because you are managing a completely different balance sheet with different goals and objectives.
- ● You have to learn a different language: earn-out, grantor trust, market volatility, yield to maturity, lifetime exemption, generation skipping, UBTI, cap-rate, GRAT, and a little bit of Greek, alpha and beta.
- ● You must shuffle and restructure the team, since you are now playing a different game with different assets and different goals for different stakeholders.
- ● You ask yourself a key question: "Do I need an asset manager, a wealth manager, or a family office?"

THE SALE OF A business can be a lot like experiencing a hurricane. The winds explode in intensity, every aspect of your life is impacted, and every decision is an emotional negotiation. Then, the next day, the sea is calm and the sun comes out in the form of a large deposit in your bank account. But now there are all these remaining assets and issues scattered everywhere. How do you start the process of cleanup? And how do you find your new *why*, if you haven't found it already?

With this chapter, we'll navigate the waters of your personal finances post-transaction—with an eye on your personal lifestyle as well as generational wealth considerations. Yes, the stakeholder list has shortened to you, your family, and perhaps your chosen charities. You want to make sure that your family can live and work comfortably for generations to come, and preferably without entitling them. Another of my favorite concepts from Warren Buffett, which is his intent to leave his kids "enough money so they can do anything, but not so much that they can do nothing."[22]

On that note, we kick off this chapter with the second of the major preparations I mentioned in chapter 9: preparing the owner(s).

Anticipate the Soft Psychological Issues

The process of preparing the owner(s) revolves primarily around the soft psychological issues—all those emotions that you will experience before, during, and after the sale closes. They are all extremely important to anticipate, as they can impact the transaction while also dragging down your happiness post-transaction.

Out of all the emotions listed at the start of this chapter, the most damaging and often overlooked is the first one: separation anxiety. Over the years, you have nurtured this business much like a parent nurtures a child. You have helped develop it, instilled strong values and integrity, helped it grow to reach its highest potential, and prepared it to be self-sustaining and independent.

Unlike a parent-child relationship though, a sale transaction often represents the *complete* termination of your relationship. Once the sale happens, you no longer have the right to lead the business. This can be extremely traumatic for those who have spent their life caring for the organization, and it's also potentially traumatic in a real-world sense for the stakeholders. So, as you prepare yourself for the sale, you must first anticipate some separation anxiety, not just for you, but also for anyone who currently works in the business or depends on it as part of their life.

Next, let's discuss the insecurity you are likely to experience. Remember in chapter 4, when I mentioned how a business getting traction is like

22 Richard I Kirkland, Jr., "Should You Leave It All to the Children," *Fortune*, September 29, 1986, http://archive.fortune.com/magazines/fortune/fortune_archive/1986/09/29/68098/index.htm.

a car accelerating and merging onto the highway? Now you're approaching the opposite scenario. Now you need to prepare to downshift and take the exit ramp. You're about to come to the end of an arduous yet rewarding journey. The idea can be terrifying.

The tendency is to think of this off-ramp as a temporary situation. You start looking ahead to the next big, risky thing that will motivate you every day, reestablish the social interaction you grew accustomed to at work, and give you that sense of meaning and purpose you might feel are slipping away. In response, many sellers pre-transaction will experience eleventh-hour doubts that can blow up the deal. Post-transaction, some sellers will search for the next on-ramp and quickly return to the highway.

This can lead to a situation that often proves damaging even to entrepreneurs who have enjoyed long-term success and the security of a huge financial windfall post-transaction. If you haven't already, you might soon feel the urge to start another business. Yes, you were successful with your business, and yes, the concept of becoming a serial entrepreneur is very exciting. All entrepreneurs have that mix of ego, confidence, and thrill-seeking that got them to where they are and that gives them confidence to believe they can easily do it all again.

Here's the thing: Some *can*! But some *can't*. And there is no guarantee which of those two camps you will fall into. Don't forget about that element of luck that served as the tailwind on your entrepreneurial journey. Luck can't be predicted or scheduled—only hoped for. And bad luck on your next venture is just as likely as good luck. We have seen it happen many times: Even the most skilled entrepreneurs can lose large chunks of their fortune on subsequent ventures that don't quite pan out.

Future businesses that aren't successful will deplete your wealth and your legacy. So, if you are thinking about starting another business, it's important to establish parameters of investment so that you don't completely wipe out the gains from your recent sale.

If the risk sounds terrifying, then it is probably best to ignore the urge to jump into another business. Besides, think about it this way: You're *already* running a new business. Your life after the sale, with all its complexities and its need for strong leadership, is *itself* a business.

After accumulating substantial wealth, there is an additional fiduciary mandate that you must recognize when managing the balance sheet for your family and heirs: wealth preservation. This concept sometimes conflicts with one's natural entrepreneurial desires. The conflicting emotions of greed and security often return in full force. To manage this conflict, the balance sheet has to be viewed and managed in its entirety with goals designed for new shareholders.

Think of your life and your family balance sheet as a holding company with various assets. You are effectively the CEO of this holding company, and you have a fiduciary responsibility to the beneficiaries, who are a combination of you, your heirs, charity, and if you don't plan properly, the IRS. So, as you take that next step into your new journey as the owner and leader of the business that is your post-transaction life and the family balance sheet, let's examine some strategies for how to run that business effectively.

Key Questions about Your New Business

If you were starting a new business today, what would be the first questions you would ask yourself about how to set it up? Many of these same questions apply to completing your pre-transaction planning and preparing yourself to face the post-business life ahead of you. They just need to be adjusted slightly to address your new reality. The goal is to answer all these questions as you design your new business plan:

- How much do I need annually to live the lifestyle to which I've grown accustomed?

- How will my balance sheet be different than it used to be? (Hint: it will be *radically* different.)
- What estate plan and trusts and other entities do we have currently? What trusts do I need to create for my family? How are they different? And who are they benefiting?
- How much do I want to give to charity?
- How should I invest the entire balance sheet, not just looking at liquid investments?
- From what entities will my family receive income?
- And finally, the key question: What team members do I have in place to assist me with Next Generation Wealth Planning and Education (NextGen Planning)?

As you can imagine, the answers to these questions are always interrelated, which adds complexity to the equation. We will spend much of this chapter and the next answering them.

Cost and Cash Flow Concerns

During pre-transaction planning, you and your all-star team performed the surgical cost-separation of your personal life from your business life. This often leaves the seller shocked about what their lifestyle actually costs. However, this is an important exercise because it calculates what proceeds of the sale of the business (plus your other assets) will be required to provide for you and your family.

Companies have a way of becoming a little like a socialist government—once you get used to the entitlements the government provides, it's not easy to take them away. Don't underestimate how far this socialism concept can spread within a company. One client we guided through the process told us before we began that his personal lifestyle expenses were about $500,000, but after our analysis, we learned that they were actually over $3.5 million. This included the cost of seven cars, health and life insurance for twenty-three extended family members, an airplane, a helicopter, lawn service for five families, bill pay for all, a handful of mysterious salaries for who knows what, and more.

Don't set yourself up for the sale without knowing how to handle the unwinding of the socialist state! Know the all-important answer to this question: Will I have enough to live on? The good news is that these expenses are all add backs to EBITDA.

Your New Commitments, Challenges, and Role

When planning for this new business that is their post-transaction life, many entrepreneurs forget to account for the time commitment this new business will require. You must understand that you are the steward of this wealth for future generations and beneficiaries. This can take time. And yes, this is estate planning.

What is estate planning? In summary, it is planning for the current and future transfer and governance of the family balance sheet in accordance with the evolving family mission and doing so efficiently through multiple generations (some of whom haven't even been born yet). Estate planning involves navigating the ever-changing tax code, managing growing and changing family structures, accounting for in-laws (and in-laws that become outlaws), anticipating changing asset composition, and allowing for changing societal norms.

The documents that direct this process include wills, trusts, business operating agreements, charitable foundations, prenups, postnups, and powers of attorney. At Waldron Private Wealth, the term we use to better describe this process and responsibility is Next Generation Wealth Planning and Education (NextGen Planning).

The continuous process of NextGen Planning has now taken over the continuous process of succession planning. Or if you transitioned the business to the next generation of leadership, then the succession plan runs *in tandem* with NextGen Planning. So, as you plan your day-to-day, you have to anticipate these roles or jobs and provide for them in your time allotment. Otherwise, anxiety will creep in, as you won't have time to pursue the passions and dreams of your next chapter. Your days won't be fulfilling; they will *come at you.*

These issues can seem logical and fact based on the surface, but there is an emotional component as well. As the CEO of this new business, you must carefully manage a balance sheet with a combination of assets, including stocks; bonds; cash; real estate (perhaps residential, commercial, and industrial); life insurance (some of it left over from the business because the buyer had no use for it); private equity positions; note receivables; escrow receivables; other small business interests; and oftentimes, significant personal assets like homes, automobiles, planes, boats, collectibles, and so on. From the technical side, you will manage and protect most of this through a collection of LLCs, S-Corporations, partnerships, trusts, and foundations.

Further, it is essential to identify the employees or team members you will need to help you execute your new fiduciary responsibility. If that sounds complicated, that's because it is. This is where a lack of NextGen Planning can cross over to frustration before leading to anxiety.

The Greed vs. Security Trap

After the transaction, you are likely to have dramatically tilted the content of your balance sheet from the illiquid business interest into cash and liquid assets. For some reason, behavioral finance fundamentals are something that sellers almost never address and advisors never bring up. But it is critically important that you understand market volatility and the radical emotional and behavioral response that volatility can cause. The irony is that entrepreneurs have experienced market volatility many times over the course of their careers; they just didn't see it in their private business value. If you're not careful, this tendency will lead you into the greed vs. security trap.

We as human beings are hardwired to make the wrong decisions in the investment arena. The emotions of security and greed can cause us to take actions that are essentially the opposite of what would be logical in a given situation. If the price of something is low, you should buy, and if the price of something is high, you should sell. But in the investment arena, unless you are trained to recognize this condition and its long-term negative impact, humans are hardwired to do exactly the opposite. This can lead to significant financial damage. To quote Warren Buffett once again, "I am fearful when others are greedy and greedy when others are fearful."[23]

Just remember that multiples for valuing private companies in all industries change all the time. In public markets, you can see it on your iPhone instantly. You have to fight the gloom and doom, hysteria, and exaggeration that the daily news will try to sell you. As an aside, this is why we refer to these cable business news shows as "financial pornography."

So how do you learn to manage the conflict of greed and security in investing? By establishing a process that helps prevent the natural human tendency of committing to the wrong action at the wrong time. But what would such a process look like?

The Lifestyle vs. Legacy Portfolio

At Waldron Private Wealth, our Lifestyle vs. Legacy Portfolio investment management approach helps our clients compartmentalize those conflicting emotions of greed and security by training the mind to

---

23 Liz Moyer, "Warren Buffett's Big Bank Score Proves His Saying True Once Again: 'Be Greedy When Others Are Fearful,'" CNBC, June 30, 2017, https://www.cnbc.com/2017/06/30/buffetts-big-bank-score-proves-be-greedy-when-others-are-fearful.html.

control the emotional extremes of greed vs. security that can arise due to market volatility.

Successful entrepreneurs have likely accumulated a family balance sheet that is greater than the amount required to provide for their lifestyle. Once we have discovered what the actual lifestyle demand is on the family assets, then we can perform our Lifestyle Legacy financial analysis. This calculation takes into account the following:

- The total family balance sheet
- How the family is taxed
- How much income is coming from illiquid assets like real estate, other private businesses, board fees, receivables, licenses or intangibles, and so on
- How much the family wants to give to heirs and to charity
- In what entities the assets are held and how they are taxed
- And of course, how much it will cost to run the lives of the senior generation

From this analysis, we can then begin to determine the portion of the family balance sheet that is required to provide for the lifestyle of the senior generation. This becomes the *Lifestyle Portfolio*. Meanwhile, the residual amount of family assets becomes the *Legacy Portfolio*. These are the family assets that will likely never be required to support the senior generation and will instead be invested for the benefit of future generations.

These two different pools of assets will be called upon to provide different benefits for different generations in different time frames, and therefore, they have different investment mandates and objectives. For instance, we typically construct the Lifestyle Portfolio to focus on income generation with the goal of lower volatility and preservation. As a result, in times of market corrections, the emotion of security rarely comes into question because the Lifestyle Portfolio has a lower volatility mandate to provide income for the senior generation. Greed does not hijack security.

Conversely, the Legacy Portfolio can assume higher volatility, given that volatility risk is reduced with longer time horizons. In fact, we teach the senior and future generations that volatility is your friend over the long term, since it gives you opportunities to deploy new capital at lower values. Volatility is why these assets tend to garner higher returns long term. In up markets, the Legacy Portfolio has its greed satisfied and its security muted. In market corrections, volatility is muted because of the opportunity for long-term benefit to future generations. The Legacy Portfolio also helps identify how and where illiquid private equity investments fit in.

Understanding the conflict of these two emotions and their potential extremes in advance of experiencing them in real time will help you avoid major mistakes and the resulting damage to the family balance sheet. If you let emotions take over during euphoric market highs and anxiety-ridden market lows, you risk making the kinds of decisions that can hamper generational wealth. In late 2009, for instance, a client came to us in search of a new advisor because they had lost confidence in the abilities of their current advisor. This wonderful couple had sold a successful business two years earlier, but on March 6th of 2009 their broker told them, "You have to get out of the stock market immediately, one hundred percent, and you have to move it all into municipal bonds." So, this nice couple did exactly that.

To put this in perspective, March 6th turned out to be the absolute lowest point in the market during the financial crisis. By the time this couple came to us, the market had already rebounded approximately 23 percent, and their broker had no plan or guidance on when to get back into the market. Here, the advisor had lost his conviction to his training and had no context of the larger picture of his clients' financial needs.

THE MARKET'S WORST AND best days tend to be clustered, which makes missing out on a handful of those days a common occurrence for investors attempting to guess when trends will begin and end. Missing those important days can have a severe effect on one's wealth in the long run.

Your Team and Its Structure

Good business leaders have developed and refined their own Velocity of Decision-Making and are used to going 100 miles per hour and relying on their gut to make decisions for their business. But now that you are looking ahead to the new business that is your family balance sheet and next generation wealth planning, the decisions you must make are many and varied. Now they impact you and your family more directly. You are likely to have less experience in these kinds of decisions, and the stakes are typically higher. With this in mind, you will want to begin exploring different teams and structures for how to manage and *preserve* your family's wealth.

There are three typical structures:

1. Do it yourself
2. Set up your own family office
3. Create a hybrid Multi-Family Office (MFO)

DISCLAIMER: Waldron Private Wealth has no specific preference for any of the above three options. We work with many family offices to augment their expertise, and we function as the family office for individuals and families who choose outsourcing to a greater degree. There is no right or wrong structure—the goal is to find the solution that is appropriate and cost-effectively meets your family's unique needs.

Do It Yourself

Here's what doing it yourself looks like:

Without Consolidated Oversight

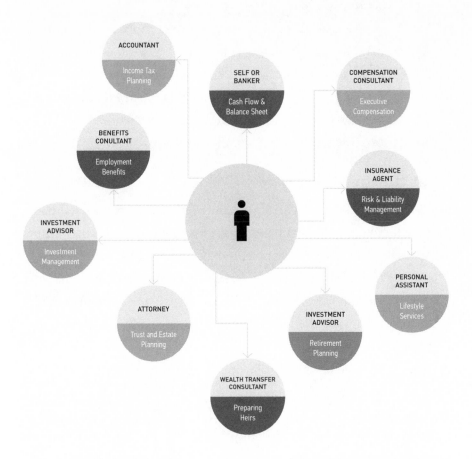

Individual advisors may be unaware of how their actions affect the whole.

For this option to be successful, three elements must all be present: you have to have the *time* for it (and be willing to spend your time this way), you have to *enjoy* it, and you have to be *good* at it.

Some choose this route as their way of staying engaged and in control. But we have seen a trend for those who choose to do it themselves. As they get older, we often get calls from them saying things like, "This is getting too complex for me," "I don't *want* to do this anymore," or "If something happens to me, what happens to my spouse and family who aren't involved with any wealth management issues?"

More people than ever before are concerned about succession risk for their financial advisor. So, they find themselves seeking out a knowledgeable, talented, and multifaceted firm—a "multi-family office"—to work with them as an advisor team, eliminating the potential successor risk presented by an individual advisor retiring.

Set Up Your Own Family Office

Studies suggest that supporting a family office requires a capital base of $400 million to $500 million on the low end. Recently, other white papers have indicated this number to be closer to $1 billion. The problem with this analysis is that it makes an unfair assumption that all family offices are created equal. This simply isn't true. "Family office" is perhaps the most overused term without any consistent definition. We have a saying at Waldron Private Wealth: "If you've seen one family office, you've seen one family office."

What you need for a family office to be effective depends on the services it provides, what the family needs it to do, the family makeup, the current balance sheet, and the family's vision for the future. Once you have reached this understanding, then you can determine what expertise is needed from the team to get you there. Finally, you must decide if you want to hire, manage, and provide benefits for some or all of that talent in a family office or outsource it.

This exercise starts differently and has different goals depending on if you are first generation, second generation, or even further out. If you are a first-generation creator of the wealth, it is a somewhat simpler undertaking because you are making this decision for the goals and needs of one family: Mom, Dad, and their heirs.

If you are from the second generation or beyond, you have to make the decision for multiple families because it is likely that assets have been transferred into multiple trusts, partnerships, LLCs, and so on. In our experience, multiple-generation families with wealth in excess of $20 million have on average of ten to fifteen such trusts and entities. For families with wealth in excess of $50 million, that number grows to twenty to twenty-five trusts and entities.

Further, these trusts and entities almost certainly cover multiple heirs or families of different sizes, locations, financial literacy, and needs—not to mention multiple stakeholders with their own emotional issues and complexities. (For those who have done this, you know exactly what I mean.) With heirs from the second generation and beyond, if you embark on this family office exercise, you must understand that there is an extra step: You have to identify what are the centralized services that all families of that generation need and what uniquely tailored services are needed by each individual family member (and there will be many). This can be an eye-opening experience for many later-generation family leaders.

When considering a family office, the seller of a business usually comes to realize that there is an executive assistant or two who manages many of the lifestyle tasks for various family members. We often run into scenarios where the CFO, controller, accounting firm, or finance department employee from the business has been providing financial and administrative services for the family. It quickly becomes obvious that, as part of the transaction, the individuals who provide these services need to continue doing so by being employed by the family.

In working with clients to help answer the question, "Should we create a family office?" we first start to help them define the vision of the future balance sheet. This loaded question tends to trigger many additional variables. Is the preference public or private securities? Equity or debt? What is the income requirement? What is the liquidity need and liquidity premium worth? How do I address diversification and allocation decisions in this future balance sheet? And what about asset location? Which trusts, partnerships, or LLCs are best suited for what type of assets? These decisions have to be considered not only for the individual but for all stakeholders, beneficiaries, and contingent beneficiaries.

Some families prefer publicly traded stocks, bonds, mutual funds, and ETFs because of the liquidity (that they never enjoyed in their own business), ease of trading, and easier due diligence and management compared to private securities. Some don't like the public markets because they don't feel they have any control over the outcome or don't like the daily visible volatility. (I say "visible" because it is there in the illiquid non-mark-to-market assets; you just can't see it—out of sight out of mind.)

Some people don't like the enhanced risk and due diligence that comes with investing in private companies. Others truly enjoy the process of analyzing, purchasing, and operating private companies and the corresponding potential return opportunities. They like getting their hands dirty and getting involved. This, however, assumes a controlled position in private companies. Others only like taking minority positions so they can avoid the day-to-day management burden.

Some families love real estate because it is tangible, and in tough times, there is still a building standing there. In addition, there's the ability to leverage its purchase and refinance its appreciation on a tax-efficient basis. If you plan to invest in real estate, then you have to decide on whether to invest in commercial, residential, industrial, or a combination and whether to diversify geographically. Will you invest directly without partners or as an LP with others? If you go without outside partners, then you need to hire or develop the expertise to analyze opportunities and then manage and lease the space. Some like to source all of those functions internally. Others like to buy and then outsource management and leasing.

If you pursue real estate investments, it is critical that you invest for total return rather than income or cash flow. Too often, we see post-transaction entrepreneurs try to replace their past income from business distributions with income from real estate. Solving for income can lead to adverse investment decisions, as a person can take on too much credit, interest, and liquidity risk just so they can reap the highest current income from the investment.

These are only some of the considerations to think about when creating a vision for the future balance sheet. We have seen everything from a heavy focus on public markets to private equity to real estate. But most often it is a combination of them all, as this provides asset diversification in support of wealth preservation. Creating this vision of the future balance sheet is a healthy and necessary exercise in determining which skill sets are needed, how often they are needed, and how to structure the management of the financial issues of the family.

After defining the future vision of the balance sheet, we can then identify the services required to manage that balance and discuss with the family other services that may be needed given their specific situation. To help with this, Waldron Private Wealth has created a Family Office Service Menu designed to guide this discussion (waldronprivatewealth.com/wp-content/uploads/2019/08/Family-Office-Service-Menu.pdf).

In our experience, we have found that these are the services most commonly provided by a family office, either through internal staff or external outsourcing. Often, this process concludes with a discussion of feasibility, the options for outsourcing, or insourcing solutions (e.g., bill pay, tax preparation, legal services), and the cost-effectiveness of each.

A Multi-Family Office (MFO)

As we begin to identify the specific tasks and services the family needs and how often, it becomes clear that some services are better outsourced. Why hire for expertise that you may only utilize 25 percent of the time? The Waldron Private Wealth business model is a Multi-Family Office (MFO) that provides à la carte wealth management services to individuals and families and family offices. For many families, working with a fifty-person firm with multiple professional disciplines and skill sets is a cost-effective alternative to receiving every service imaginable. Services of an MFO can be tailored to the family office's strengths and expertise. Or an MFO can act as the family office for the family or individual. The key is customization to the unique family needs for cost-efficiency.

That said, we have seen a few clear trends in recent years. They include the following:

OUTSOURCING

An increasing number of individuals and families have turned to outsourcing more and more services to maximize cost-efficiency. This is partly true because of trend number two, which follows: the disintegration of the family office. A business owner client of ours who never intends to sell his business summed this trend up recently: "I have a very sizable and complex business," he explained. "I have to provide for its governance and management for generations to come. I don't want to add an additional complex business, and that's what a family office is. I don't want to further complicate the management burden for the next generation."

For the first generation, we have been increasingly called in to augment the family office leadership team with our Next Generation Wealth Planning and Education services and to help with family office capacity issues as the next two generations grow up, get jobs, move to different states, get married (or divorced), have children, start new businesses, and so on. They quietly absorb the services, and therefore the capacity, of the family office.

DISINTEGRATION

The disintegration of family offices once the second partner of the matriarch/patriarch passes away is a clear trend. With the aging demographics of wealth in the United States, the reason is quite logical: It's the law of taxation and division (which, incidentally, is an interesting lesson we teach to the children of our clients in NextGen Planning). The law is as follows: If the matriarch and patriarch have a net worth of, for example, $200 million, and the estate tax at 40 percent is approximately $80 million (for the purposes of this example, we're assuming no planning to mitigate), then there is a net $120 million for the heirs post-tax. Then, if there are four children, each of them equally receives $30 million. By the way, a subtle expectation-teaching lesson here for the child is that the law of taxation and division means that you can't aspire to the same lifestyle of your parents with inheritance alone. Setting expectations is a huge part of this education.

For it to make financial sense to maintain the family office, all children would need to agree to remain and bear the cost. Due to different needs, beneficiaries living in different states or countries, different-sized families and demands, and the resulting variance in perspectives on necessary services, this rarely happens. Plus, there's the big one: How do you divide the cost of the family office? Then there is the second big one: Who runs the family office and manages the team? For all of these reasons, there is a trend toward dissolution of family offices in generational transition.

PRIVATE BUSINESS INVESTING

The next trend is that more families are identifying a mission to directly (or through "club deals") invest in private businesses. These families tend to want to work with in-house investment banking professionals with deep merger and acquisition experience. This provides the core infrastructure and overhead coverage for these family offices, which usually require at least $1 billion in family net worth to support the cost of internal investment banking skills within the family office.

Smaller family offices use an affiliation of investment bankers familiar with their industry and size preferences and refer them opportunities to minimize the internal cost burden. Private equity–focused investment makes this kind of family office especially susceptible to the dissolution trend above.

Solving for Your Goals

With comprehensive strategic counsel, you will understand the challenge ahead of managing the entire balance sheet of different assets and liabilities for multiple generations. Hopefully, you have determined the best team and structure for managing the family's wealth. Now it is time to develop goals and set your investment objectives. Remember the business school lesson, "That which gets measured gets accomplished." The key question then is against what metric do you measure your progress? This is the *performance* of your assets on an after-tax basis.

It confounds me how people—and especially professionals in our industry—discuss and measure progress toward goals exclusively in terms of *return*. However, *performance* is not just a numeric rate of return. It is comprised of two components: the rate of return and the level of *risk* taken to generate that return. For example, if I received a 9 percent rate of return and my neighbor received an 8 percent rate of return without further data, one would naturally prefer the 9 percent return. However, if you could achieve the 8 percent return while taking only 70 percent of the risk required to achieve the 9 percent return, most people would prefer the 8 percent return. Focusing on the numeric return without consideration for the amount of risk taken is dangerous. It's like flying blind. We have seen major damage inflicted on wealth resulting from this lack of understanding.

The key is to design a plan based on the knowledge of all assets and liabilities, the amount of income needed, and the source of that income. Then, when you have defined all this, you discuss and pressure-test the plan in advance of real-time volatility.

Hierarchy of Factors Contributing to Investment Decisions

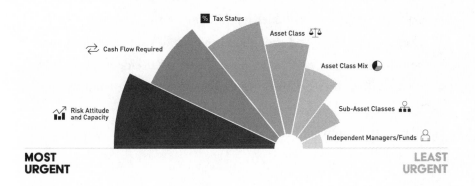

A byproduct of this analysis is what we refer to as "solving for your goals." This is a concept we developed that serves as a far better measuring stick for asset performance. The proper calculation should be based on all the facts and circumstances of your unique situation (i.e., how much you have, how much demand is placed on those assets to generate income for family members, how much liquidity is needed, what liabilities or contingent liabilities exist, how you are taxed, how much you want to give to charity, and *all of the other aspects* of your financial life). From this analysis, we can then build a lifestyle and legacy allocation strategy designed to support your goals with full knowledge of the risk inherent in the allocation.

It blows my mind when I see people compare their return, not *performance*, against an index like the S&P or the Dow or the World Index that has absolutely no relevance to their personal situation. You need to calculate and measure against your specific goals.

Emotional Lessons:

- Avoid the greed vs. security trap. As the balance sheet transitions, understand the dangerous inverse interaction of these two emotions in the process of managing the investment of the balance sheet, especially liquid securities. Understand it and control it.
- Conduct a detailed and thoughtful analysis of your needs and goals, and then listen to your inner voice when you decide whether to do it yourself, set up a family office, or work with a multifamily office.
- Set all biases and relationships aside and go through the same decision matrix you would use with any other business decision.

Technical Strategies:

- Accept your new position as president of this new "family holding company."
- Define the vision for the new balance sheet and define the goals for the family.
- Calculate your Lifestyle Portfolio and Legacy Portfolio needs.
- Go through the analytical process to answer the question: Do I need an asset manager, wealth manager, a family office, or some combination of the three?
- Identify which family office services the family will need to help them achieve their goals and define how progress will be measured.
- Don't fall into the dangerous trap of measuring *return* instead of *performance*.

- Calculate and measure to solve for your goals.

Proper Sequencing Is Key

I'll close by highlighting one final point about the technical strategies above: Approach this challenge in the proper sequence. Without proper sequencing, you could wind up putting the wrong people in the wrong roles.

Take the time soon after the business is sold—or before, if possible—to determine what your family's needs are. Once this is done, you can analyze which wealth management structure best suits your situation.

Do this without thinking of any service professionals or firms that you are currently using, because any personal relationships you have developed might prejudice the analysis and cause you to put them on the team before you can properly assess what your needs are and who would be best for the role. Once you determine the best structure and services required, go back and consider current and other professionals who have the skill set and expertise that would best help your family manage their wealth and achieve their goals. It is highly likely that some of the current relationships will have a role on the new team structure. Approaching this challenge in the correct sequence will allow you to come to an objective, unbiased decision.

Many times, we have seen people approach this decision in the opposite order. They have a team of advisors that they have used for years, and they retrofit their structure to fit the advisors and relationships, agnostic of skills, capabilities, and capacity. At best, this approach creates inefficiencies and frustration. Remember, managing the balance sheet is like running a business. It's like Jim Collins says: "Get the right people on the bus. Get the right people in the right seat."[24]

---

24 Jim Collins, *Good to Great: Why Some Companies Make the Leap . . . and Others Don't* (New York: HarperBusiness, 2011).

CHAPTER ELEVEN

Preparing the Heirs

Stakeholders:

- ✔ You
- ✔ Your spouse
- ✔ Your heirs

Emotions and Symptoms:

- ✔ Feeling that reality has become surreal
- ✔ Anticipation for the discovery of the next chapter of life
- ✔ Sense of loss of relationships and position
- ✔ Excitement for reconnection with other relationships and interests

IT'S BEEN A LONG journey that peaked with a hurricane, but now here you are on open water. There is nothing but blue sky and pristine ocean ahead of you. The seas are calm, and the wind is still. It's kind of a surreal moment. The transaction closes with a shot of excitement and adrenaline initiated by the culmination of an extremely difficult and emotionally challenging negotiation: the wire transfer. If you have done the pre-transaction planning on these issues, then *some* of the technical and financial matters will be easier to deal with.

For those who have *emotionally* prepared for the Day-After Phase, we have reached the beginning of the next chapter of your life—a day to celebrate and to feel energized about the future. For those who haven't *emotionally* prepared, the Day After can be scary, even downright terrifying. If you don't know what comes next, then your daily life can feel jarring and you may hit a wall—you were going 100 miles per hour with your business and its transition, and now suddenly your speedometer drops to zero. I have seen this lead to depression, mourning, loneliness, and in some extreme situations, marriage problems, health problems, and substance abuse issues.

We have discussed the process of deciding how you identify and structure the financial, tax, trust, legal, investment, and lifestyle services that the family needs. And we reviewed our process for answering the all-important question: What is the most cost-efficient balance between outsourcing and internal sourcing? Finally, we discussed whether you should go it alone, establish a family office, or go with a hybrid model. Unfortunately, many sellers make the mistake of assuming that once the business has been sold and the decisions have been made, their work is done.

What they're forgetting is that their new business will continue to require their attention. There is, after all, still the family balance sheet to manage.

Proper Next Generation Wealth Planning and Education has two steps:

1. Prepare the wealth for the heirs (the hard issues)
2. Prepare the heirs for the wealth (the soft issues)

Preparing the heirs for the eventual task of managing wealth is the most important of the soft issues. Putting considerable wealth under the control of someone unprepared to deal with it creates an extremely dangerous situation. As a classic example, consider the statistic that 78 percent of NFL players are bankrupt a mere five years out of football.[25]

---

25 Pablo S. Torre, "How (And Why) Athletes Go Broke," *Sports Illustrated*, March 23, 2009.

Without sufficient personal instruction, you wouldn't allow your child to drive a car, shoot a gun, or navigate your boat into the open ocean. Handing them considerable wealth without properly training them could be just as dangerous!

We have noticed a growing concern among our clients about the lack of preparedness of their children to deal with the wealth they will receive. Recently, this has become one of the top priorities of our clients. At the same time, next to succession planning, talking to their children and grandchildren about wealth is the area they most often *avoid*. There are three reasons we have observed this to be true:

1. They know it is extremely important, but they also recognize that it isn't their skill set.
2. They know that the subject is highly emotional, and if not handled properly, it could have some extreme unintended consequences.
3. They do not know the answer to the key question about full disclosure: Should we pretend that we aren't as wealthy as we are, or should we be transparent with our children and grandchildren and disclose the full picture of our wealth?

AS AN ASIDE TO number two, recently we were engaged to work with the children of a longtime client to help integrate, communicate, and educate them on NextGen Planning. As we were educating them about the purpose of trusts, tax efficiency, asset protection, and so on, one of the children (who was forty-eight years old at the time) said, "I thought the reason for a trust was that our parents didn't *trust us*!" Scary unintended consequences.

Regarding full disclosure about family wealth, the main argument we've heard against it is this: "We don't want our children to feel entitled or take away their motivation to work." While we have many, many stories to challenge this argument, this one captures it best:

One of our clients was firmly set against disclosure. He sold his business, and soon after, there was an article in the local *Business Times* that reported on the sale and estimated the value of the business at $300 million. (This was an accurate report, by the way.) So I asked this client, "Do you think your children and grandchildren saw this?"

"No," he said. "They don't read the *Business Times*."

"Have you ever heard of Google?" I asked him.

"Why?" he said.

As we sat there, I googled his name and company name, and that same *Business Times* article, among others, populated the first page.

"You know," I said, "this article doesn't mention that $300 million was the enterprise value before $100 million of debt. Nor does it mention the $75 million of taxes you had to pay."

"Huh," the client said.

I explained that by not educating his heirs about family wealth and the related financial issues, he was exacerbating the condition that he was trying to prevent. So, beware of the "Google effect." It used to be that you could hide wealth from your kids. But these days, you can find out just about anything using Google. (And simply because it's published online does not mean it's accurate.) Ask yourself, would you rather tell them in the context of education and responsibility that comes with wealth or have them try to piece it together for themselves?

Within weeks of our discussion, we were holding sessions with the children and grandchildren of our Google-averse client to educate them on technical, financial, tax, trust, investment, and other concepts with permission for full disclosure. Interestingly, to start our session, we asked them to write down what they thought their parents and grandparents were worth. Thanks to Google, they estimated twice the actual number.

> **FAMILIES WITH EXPOSURE TO** publicly traded companies are particularly susceptible to having their net worth easily accessible online, as public companies are required to publish reports that detail who their significant shareholders are and how many shares they own.

Balancing Your New Lifestyle with Time, Money, and Energy

You may have noticed that with these final chapters, we have returned to a much shorter list of stakeholders. This is because, as we come to the end of our journey, it is time to focus on you and your immediate family. Assuming that your sale or transition has accounted for all the stakeholders associated with your business, and assuming that you've properly planned for both the hard and soft issues of generational wealth management, it's time to think about you.

Another trend we've seen develop is that clients are favoring strategies that help them *simplify* their lives, even as their considerable wealth allows them to keep adding more and more components to their lifestyles.

At the age of forty-four, a close friend sold his successful business. Of course, he tried to stick around in a role with the succeeding business, but that didn't last, as usual. At his age, he was filled with energy and excitement to experience life. He directed that energy into an additional home in Florida (and another home each for his parents and in-laws), a plane, and a yacht. At the peak, he owned two planes, three boats, and nine houses and had countless employees in two states and on the boats. He bought the house next to him so he could store supplies for his main home. It looked like a Home Depot with aisles set up, and supplies inventoried and labeled. Light bulbs were in aisle seven.

For the next ten years, this couple enjoyed time with their family and friends (a group that Maureen and I are privileged to be a part of), traveling the world and floating around the Caribbean. The support staff that was required to sustain this lifestyle was considerable; the payroll they had to manage was likely higher than that of many small companies.

Then I began to notice them starting the sizing down, or simplification, process. My friend sold much of his personal real estate, reduced his auto fleet, cut down on his travel schedule, and traded the yacht for a smaller boat, one without the need for a captain, first mate, or crew.

He is not alone in this trend. In fact, a high percentage of our clients follow this same path, which we call right-sizing their lifestyle. Post-sale they have more time, resources, and energy, so they add complexity. Soon after, they learn (sometimes the hard way) that such a lifestyle is stressful to manage and therefore *reduces* contentment. Most clients, at some point or another, wind up sizing down and simplifying. They optimize their lifestyle so it reduces the stress to a manageable level while also maximizing their enjoyment. It gives them back quality time.

So how do you do that (preferably without having to sacrifice too much of the lifestyle you've grown accustomed to)? It starts by flipping an old adage on its head . . .

Rent vs. Buy

Quick disclaimer before we begin this one: Everything is of course guided by personal preference, but this is a real trend we are seeing . . .

All your life, you've been counseled that it's almost always better to buy than rent. Buying is how you build wealth, while renting is like throwing money away. But now that you have *achieved* wealth, the way to maintain the best, least stressful, and sometimes, the most cost-efficient lifestyle is to rent anything and everything you can. Here's the shorthand for why this works:

Buying = maintenance, upkeep, and most times, the management of additional staff

Renting = outsourcing all that stress and expense to someone else

And here are a few examples of assets that people are choosing to rent instead of buy:

SECONDARY HOMES

When you're not in the home, you have to pay someone to manage it, and when you *are* in it, there's all that staff and maintenance that applies to your primary residence. We're seeing many clients opt for the location flexibility of vacation clubs like Exclusive Resort, Inspirato, or upscale hotels (whenever and wherever they choose). Instead of managing a staff, they prefer to enjoy all the amenities and the concierge services in many different locations. Hand someone else the keys and the list of maintenance issues that come with it. At first glance, renting seems expensive, but when we do the math:

{Hard cost + opportunity cost} / days spent per year = daily use cost
Renting looks really good!

CARS

There's no need to keep the small sports car(s). Someday soon, you won't even be able to get into it anymore!

AIRCRAFT

When working with our clients, we do the break-even analysis of the average hours that they fly and the nature of their trips to determine their personal best approach: own outright vs. fractional shares vs. jet card vs. charter. Prior to purchasing an aircraft, many of our clients are unaware of the sheer expense and upkeep related to owning. For some people, oftentimes those still running an active business, ownership makes sense. For others, the question is why commit to any of that when you can buy a fractional share from Flexjet or NetJets or simply charter a plane when you need one? This gives you aircraft options for different types of trips while leaving the aircraft management headaches to someone else.

BOATS

We often say that the best two days of a boat-owner's life are the day he or she buys the boat and the day he or she sells it. Here's another area where renting or chartering usually makes much more sense. It's the same equation as above.

HEALTHCARE

You might not have considered this one, but working with a patient advisory firm like PinnacleCare can drastically simplify the complexities of our ever-changing healthcare system, particularly if you have a complicated diagnosis. Many people are turning to patient advisory firms to help manage the headaches associated with the most valuable asset of their life: their health.

YOUR PRIMARY RESIDENCE

We close with an eye-opening one. People who love to travel like to simplify their living and opt to rent a condo. For others, the primary residence is the only remaining asset where they're willing to tolerate the necessary maintenance and management. Personally, I don't think Maureen and I will ever sell our home, even though we live in four rooms of the twelve. Too many memories there. But we do have a condo in Grand Cayman for easy living.

Your Emotional Well-Being

As you create your Day-After plan, consider the three nonfinancial elements of your lifestyle that you will want to keep in balance. Think of them as three interlocking circles:

The first circle encompasses your social life. Yes, you're now going to have more time with your family, but you're also going to be dealing with the loss of some of the relationships and social connections you used to enjoy every day (sometimes without even thinking about them). If you're like most longtime business owners, most of the people you know are from the business. Now that you're not seeing these people every day, how do you fill the gaps in the socialization time you were accustomed to? How do you ensure that you still get to spend time with your friends, even if most of them are either still associated with your business or otherwise at work? On the flip side, how do you rebalance expectations with the people in your family who now get to spend much more time with you than they are used to? Don't underestimate these factors, as they will contribute greatly to how much you enjoy your Day-After lifestyle.

The next circle, emotional and intellectual stimulation, addresses the question of how you will keep yourself engaged without the business. When Dick Jenrette (the "J" in DLJ) passed away, he left a list of handwritten life lessons. One of the entries was, "Stay intellectually engaged." In the early days, you worked eighty-hour weeks to get your business off the ground. Then you poured your heart and soul into keeping the business growing sustainably. During the Transition Phase, you had to dedicate a huge portion of your emotional and intellectual attention to getting the best deal in the sale or transition. Now, suddenly, all of that is gone. How will you occupy your time? How will you keep yourself sharp? How will you stay engaged?

The final circle is about your sense of purpose. For a long time, you have identified as a business owner. It is how you defined yourself (both in your own mind and to others), and as such, it has become the foundation of your identity. After you're no longer running the business, you might find yourself struggling with many self-identity and self-esteem issues. How do you define who you are if you're no longer a business owner? Further, how can you give your life meaning—on a daily basis, long term, and even after you're gone?

It takes some effort and soul searching to answer these questions, but the benefits are considerable. Start by answering the question of what brings you happiness, joy, and fulfillment. If you have one, the best resource is your family vision. If you don't have one, consider the following list of possibilities:

- Spend more time with family
- Become a teacher, mentor, or coach
- Sit on advisory or executive boards
- Offer consulting services
- Pursue a hobby like fishing, tennis, golf, or hunting
- Volunteer
- Write a book
- Travel
- Pursue the next business

One client who sold a business decided that his Day-After goal was to pursue learning for the sake of learning. Today, twenty-five years after selling his business, and at the age of seventy-four, this client is learning Spanish.

Another couple who recently sold their business is sailing their boat around the world.

Another client taught entrepreneurship at Miami of Ohio University and Babson for over fifteen years. At eighty years old, he still sits on the board of Miami of Ohio.

One of my favorite clients is the former chairman of the FCC and the founding managing partner of a prominent DC law firm. He is eighty-four years old and is showing no signs of slowing down. To him, "staying engaged" means "staying in." This doesn't work for everyone, but it's okay for him because he achieved balance long ago between work, tennis, church, and his main priority, family.

A big part of the social, emotional, and intellectual engagement revolves around finding balance in your life. The best mix is a lifestyle that allows for family time, free time, and intellectually stimulating activities (provided they don't encroach too harshly on that equally important free time). These days, people are focused on staying in the game longer, helping to run their business even after they transition out, and dedicating time to serving on boards or engaging with philanthropic organizations.

We began this journey with an exploration of the emotional side of wealth—examining the Emotional Intelligence (EI) it takes to balance a business and all the stresses and rewards that come with it. Now we turn that EI on your personal life. Here is where we anticipate what you can expect on the personal side during the Day-After phase. Attending to the wealth and family legs of the stool will pay huge dividends, but it is also critically important to focus on yourself—your health, your intellectual engagement, and your emotional well-being. Get all of these components into balance, and you will achieve the happy, fulfilling life you have worked so hard for.

Planning, both financially and emotionally, for the Day After is extremely important. Just ask someone who didn't invest the time to do it in advance. When we take calls from new prospective clients, many of them say something similar: "We closed on the sale of our business last week, and we need to start planning for what to do next." It is not an impossible task, but it does represent an opportunity lost for addressing these critical issues early.

Enhancing the Personal Experience *and* the Financial Result

DURING MY THIRTY-SIX YEARS of advising entrepreneurs, I have realized that dealing with these highly personal and perplexing matters takes a tremendous amount of time, energy, patience, and emotion (both positive and negative). The pursuit of happiness is as unique to each of us as our thumbprint, but these two elements are consistent: You have the *money*, but you also need the *time*. As we age, I have witnessed the interpersonal reshuffling of these priorities in almost every person I have had the pleasure of working with. That reshuffling looks like this: As we get older (or more financially secure), *time* becomes more precious than *money*. Yes, preserving wealth is important, but having the time to experience the life you want is priceless.

This thirty-six-year education has made me realize that the biggest value we can provide to our clients is to give them the ability to pursue the things that they value most by giving them back more time.

A common characteristic in clients who come to us is the feeling of stress and anxiety related to the time commitment that naturally comes with increasing wealth. As I have said before, as wealth increases, so does the complexity of the issues associated with it. Needs change, the stakes get higher, and there are more and more stakeholders impacted by the outcome.

This is exactly why we have built our unique value proposition around giving our clients back their time, free from the stress and anxiety of wealth management by providing a process for:

- Development of a comprehensive strategy with a broader team, integrating tax planning, estate planning, investment, cash flow, debt, risk management, philanthropy, and all of the other components of your financial life. The team oversees the execution of the strategy with other professional team members, including accountants, attorneys, investment bankers, and commercial bankers.
- The timely identification of new risks and opportunities that creep into the picture
- Vetting alternative solutions

Many financial advisors provide professional services to families of wealth. Some offer an efficient, customizable option between doing it themselves and creating a family office. But few recognize the equal importance of the emotional side of wealth. This is the critical knowledge that allows you to balance your family's needs related to *money*, and just as importantly, with *time*.

I often ask entrepreneurs when they are deep into the Maturation Phase or have just closed their Transition, "So, if you could go back and do it all again, what would you have done differently?" As many times as I have asked that question, no one has ever said, "I would have spent less time with my family and more with the business." Instead, at their most introspective moments, they say exactly the opposite.

I learned this lesson early on and have always tried to maintain the self-awareness and self-control it takes to leave work for the family event or to schedule a date night. I know it has likely cost me significant income, growth, and value over the years, but ultimately, it was worth every penny. Remember, no matter where you find yourself on the Entrepreneurial Lifecycle, the most precious commodity is time.

Acknowledgments

NO JOURNEY IS TRAVELED alone! I have so many stakeholders to be thankful for.

I would like to thank all of the clients who have given me the privilege of counseling them through the various phases of their amazing journeys. I truly appreciate the trust and confidence they have placed in me and my firm. Particularly, I would like to thank Eddie Teraskiewicz and Dick Wiley, who were my first clients and took a chance on a young accountant who ventured out with only a vision and a loan.

I would also like to thank the entire team at Waldron Private Wealth for all their support and belief. Specifically Jeff Howden, Matt Helfrich, Chris Roe, and Mike Krol, who were instrumental early on when the firm was just a vision.

And most of all, I would like to thank my wife, Maureen, for her unconditional love and support in every aspect of my journey. She kept me on the emotional rails and always knew exactly when my confidence needed a little extra reinforcement.

Do I Need an Investment Manager, Wealth Manager, or Family Office?

By Michael Krol, CFP®, CPA, Partner and Head of Wealth Advisory

CONFUSION CREATED BY THE financial marketplace over terminology like "wealth management" and "family-office" has created a great challenge for families who seek investment management, wealth management or family office services. It has become increasingly difficult to find the services specifically relevant to an individual's or family's needs; this challenge becomes further complicated because those needs can change quite significantly as wealth accumulates. We refer to these phenomena as the Wealth Accumulation Continuum. The key for an individual or family at any stage along the continuum is to recognize their changing needs and to make sure they are asking potential providers the right questions.

> "THE KEY FOR AN INDIVIDUAL OR FAMILY AT ANY STAGE ALONG THE CONTINUUM IS TO RECOGNIZE THEIR CHANGING NEEDS AND TO MAKE SURE THEY ARE ASKING POTENTIAL PROVIDERS THE RIGHT QUESTIONS."

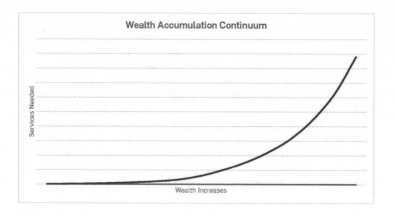

BEGINNING TO ACCUMULATE WEALTH >> INVESTMENT MANAGEMENT

When a family begins accumulating wealth, the first and most basic service they will need is investment management. Early on, it is not unusual for an individual to "self-manage" his or her investments. As the size of the investment accounts grow, however, we recommend asking the following three questions:

1. Do I have time to manage my own investments?
2. Am I good at managing my own investments?
3. Do I enjoy managing my own investments?

If the answer to any of these questions is no, an alternative approach is to hire one or more investment managers and allocate funds to each. In hiring investment managers, one should first set the overall strategic investment plan to identify the number and types of investment managers needed. We then recommend matching specific investment account mandates to managers that specialize in those particular areas. In evaluating potential investment managers, one should assess both: 1) qualitative factors, such as philosophy, process and people, and 2) quantitative factors, such as return and risk analytics over various market cycles. It is also important to understand the nature and amount of the fees you will be paying. In many cases, this will be difficult to assess because fees may be charged in the form of commissions, advisory fees or underlying product fees. Some of these fees are reported in periodic statements and some are not. This can be one of the most opaque areas of hiring an investment manager, so be sure to request and receive clarity on this topic.

ACCUMULATING SIGNIFICANT WEALTH >> WEALTH MANAGER

As wealth grows, so do the complexities and the need for additional services. At some point, a family often finds themselves with multiple investment managers or a very large sum of money which they are managing on their own. This is when it makes sense to consider a wealth manager to assist with the increased complexities and choices. A wealth manager is multi-faceted and provides services relevant to significant wealth, such as:

1. Developing an overall investment plan which aligns with family goals, required return, risk tolerance and capacity, unique tax situation and various other personal circumstances.
2. Implementing the investment plan by allocating funds amongst various investment managers, while performing ongoing manager due diligence and fund re-allocation.
3. Providing other relevant ongoing services, including cash-flow planning, tax and estate coordination, philanthropic planning, education planning, corporate benefits planning and risk management, among others.

In the absence of a wealth manager, an individual will often find him or herself in the middle of these various complexities, evaluating investment managers, and trying to make appropriate, "multi-dimensional" decisions that are impacted by cash flow, income tax, investment strategy, risk management and estate planning considerations. This can be a difficult predicament because the expertise required to effectively navigate such decisions is significantly greater than that required to navigate investment decisions alone.

In hiring a wealth manager, we recommend identifying the services beyond investment management that are relevant to your wealth and goals. Then one should evaluate a potential wealth manager based upon their expertise in providing the services required and the cost of providing these services.

> "IN HIRING A WEALTH MANAGER, WE RECOMMEND IDENTIFYING THE SERVICES BEYOND INVESTMENT MANAGEMENT THAT ARE RELEVANT TO YOUR WEALTH AND GOALS."

A wealth manager's fee may be based upon a percent of assets under management, a percent of net worth, a flat fee or a combination of the three. Many wealth managers are regulated by the Securities and Exchange Commission as a "fiduciary," and therefore are always required to act in the best interest of their clients. Conversely, other types of financial institutions, including many of those that advertise "wealth management" services, may be subject to a different set of regulations that are more lax in their requirements. In hiring a wealth manager, one should always ask how the advisor is regulated and if the firm is subject to the "fiduciary" standard.

How much wealth is needed for a family office to make sense?

At very significant levels of wealth, an individual may hear that a family office might be the right solution. Family offices exist in as many varieties as the families they represent. A true "family office" is created when such significant wealth is present, generally over $300 million, that it is cost-effective for families to hire employees who work exclusively for them. However, the reality is that family offices are a blend of services provided by in-house staff with other services outsourced to professional service firms.

We have identified over 100 different services, which a wealthy family may require, but even the wealthiest families will not find it cost-effective to hire a full-time staff with the requisite expertise to perform all of these services. For this reason, we recommend performing a full assessment of each of the possible services to determine if:

1. The individual or family has the in-house expertise to provide the service in a cost-effective manner, or
2. The service will be provided by a professional service firm, or
3. The service is not needed at this time, but will be continually evaluated for applicability

An equally important step after assessing each particular service is developing a blueprint to coordinate all of the services needed. Without this strategic blueprint and fully integrated execution, even the best team of internal staff and outside professionals can allow great opportunities to go by the wayside, while permitting significant risks to slip under the radar.

An investment manager, wealth manager, or family office may be the right choice for you. The key is to identify the services relevant to your wealth and to make sure that you are asking the right questions of potential providers.

To view the Waldron Private Wealth Family Office Service Menu, visit:

waldronprivatewealth.com/wp-content/uploads/2019/08/Family-Office-Service-Menu.pdf

About the Author

JOHN J. WALDRON graduated from Robert Morris University in 1982. He began his public accounting career in the Miami office of Price Waterhouse, where he focused on tax and other financial planning matters for privately held companies and their owners, domestic and international trust planning, and business consulting.

John left Price Waterhouse and took a position with Deloitte in Pittsburgh in 1986. At Deloitte he continued his domestic and international tax work for business owners and was part of a national executive financial planning practice. In this capacity, he managed the financial planning and investment affairs for many of the top executives and board members of the world's largest audit and tax clients and owners of closely held businesses.

In 1990, John left his career in public accounting to pursue his entrepreneurial instincts and create a unique wealth management practice, integrating an independent investment management service into the complex financial, tax, and family lives of his clientele.

John built Waldron Private Wealth based on his firm conviction that a thorough understanding of a client's entire financial picture and their unique goals must be in place before effective financial advice can be given. At the time, the independent fee-based and consultative service model he developed was disruptive to the financial planning and investment management industries, but now, that model is what most firms aspire to follow. This model has helped Waldron Private Wealth earn national recognition, including being named the #1 Wealth Advisor in Pennsylvania in *Forbes* 2019 Best in State rankings and being one of only twelve firms nationwide ranking in *Barron's* Top 100 Independent Financial Advisors each of the thirteen years the rankings have been published.

John lives in Nevillewood, Pennsylvania, with his wife, Maureen. In the winter they enjoy spending time at their home in Grand Cayman. Their preferred activities include traveling, tennis, scuba diving, bike riding, boating, and working out.